Mayhem,
Murder
&
Multi-Lets

FRANCIS DOLLEY

www.mayhemmurderandmultilets.com

Copyright

In memory of Peter Thurlow
Who didn't quite make it to read this book

Reviews

"This is an essential read. Francis' perception of property investing is highly entertaining, educational and inspiring in equal measures. It perfectly captures the tragic hysteria that sometimes permeates the human race, especially landlord-tenant relationships! It also opens the door to an established but little known system that Francis has now made his own."

Vicki Wusche
Author, Mentor, Investor
www.thesourcersapprentice.com

"This is the funniest book on property investing you're ever likely to read. It's also the most informative, knowledgeable and helpful too! Francis Dolley shows you how to cope with unexpected murder and mayhem from your tenants and still stay smiling!"

Stephanie J. Hale
Bestselling Author
www.celebrityauthorssecrets.com

Managing tenants can be a fascinating study into your own ability to withstand some of the ups and downs of being a property investor, when situations do not go to plan. What really sets a good landlord apart is how you deal with those situations. Francis has been able to stay positive even when dealing with even the most shocking of circumstances. If you rent a property in any way shape or form you MUST buy this book."

Susannah Cole
Investor, Mentor, Speaker
www.thegoodpropertycompany.co.uk

"Don't be fooled by the crazy fun title of this book. It is full of absolute gems that will save you loads of time and buckets of money as a landlord. It also gives an overview of an underground investing system that is guaranteed to fast track you from employed to entrepreneur status in record breaking time. Some books you just HAVE to read".

Iain Wallis
Chartered Accountant.
Bestselling Author and Public Speaker.
www.iainwallis.com

"As property professionals with over 14 years' experience we thought we had done and seen most things. The 'Mayhem' section of the book had us rolling about on the floor and literally laughing out loud! We were so impressed with the 'Multi-Let' section that we contacted Francis and we are now combining our talents to create an awesome training product. Buy this book, you will love it!"

Peter Licourinos and James May
Prospect Lettings,
Berkshire Investors Club & Hosts of Reading PIN
www.prospectinvestorsclub.co.uk

"Just when I thought this was a book full of (very funny) anecdotes, it took a turn and laid out an overview of a property investing system that most people would dismiss as too good to be true. After doing some research of my own I would say don't make that mistake when YOU read this book!"

Daniel Wagner
www.danielwagner.com

"As someone who has been an active investor and a landlord for more than 15 years, this book really resonated with me. Instead of the usual fodder of pretending everything is plain sailing, Francis brings the realities of

5

the property business out into the open so that the reader is prepared for anything. This book is long overdue. Having Francis' knowledge and experience at your disposal is invaluable and will help anyone who is considering wealth building through property. His warm and personal writing style makes a jam-packed essential guide highly entertaining as well - great read!"

Sophie Bennett
Author and Mentor
www.moneybondage.com

"There are some 'How to make money' books that just sit on the shelf, having seemed like a good idea at the time. Don't make that mistake here - please! I've been on the Multi-Let Cashflow System course & it's such a great concept, delivered with lovely humour and showing their in-depth knowledge. Buy this insightful, highly entertaining book; implement the teaching and watch the Cashflowing in! Highly recommended".

Vinden Grace MSc BSc (Hons) MIoD F IDM MBILD
Property Investor & Mentor
www.gkcproperty.com

"Want to get into buying high Cash flowing properties but wonder what it's really going to be like? Francis Dolley tells it like it is - warts and all. This book talks through the realities of being an HMO landlord and the problems you are likely to face along the way, how to deal with those problems and still make a decent profit. A must read for anyone wanting to understand how a property business really works."

Ant Lyons
Editor, Your Property Network
www.yourpropertynetwork.co.uk

6

A Beginning

Wherever you are in life there is no doubt that it has been a great spider's web of events and a million microscopic and compounded choices that has brought you there. Maybe, like me, you realised one day that you wanted to be altogether somewhere different and perhaps like me you used property investing to get you there. Whatever you do, life will undoubtedly forever be trying to trip you up and throw obstacles across your path. I hope that this book may inspire you to deal with the good, the bad and the ugly, and whatever else life hurls at you with a smile, while at the same time slowly and surely building a passive income through property that will enable you and your family to escape the daily grind and perhaps to even create the life of your dreams as it is doing for me.

In 2010 I stumbled upon a system that I describe as the 'Lottery Winners approach to investing'! Some people dismissed it as too good to be true and I almost did as well, but along with my daughter Emily, and to be honest, almost in desperation, we decided to 'give it a try'. The following six months were a steep learning curve like no other I have ever experienced, but we were very successful in quickly creating a monthly NET Cash flow of £5,000 that without doubt changed the direction of our lives forever and opened up many more doors of opportunities.

The good news is that we have now honed, refined and bottled up the process and have in fact now helped many people do exactly the same as we have (but often in a much shorter time and without all the pain and embarrassment we experienced while trying to find our way in the dark!) Many of these people have now become our good friends and form part of the brilliant support MLCS (explained later) community that has developed and flourished over the last few years.

Like all journeys mine began many years earlier when I fell into being a landlord. You may be aware of the term 'accidental landlord' being bandied about in recent years, referring to people who by no choice of their own found themselves stuck with a rented property and tenants to deal with. Well I was more of an 'incidental landlord', which was more than likely the cause of my two years of absolute Mayhem when I first began investing. I'll tell you why.

Contents

Books

... and their place in the world

Writing a book is no mean feat (for me anyway!). To get all that jumbled up information out of your head and down onto paper is only half of the battle, you then have a multitude of extremely harrowing undertakings if you are to stand any chance of holding the finished article in your hand. If not for the utterly brilliant Stephanie J Hale all these words would still undoubtedly be rattling around in my head. Steph made the whole process simple and relatively painless and I am really looking forward to working together on book number two, and three, and ...

Whenever I have a new book I always spend a few minutes turning it over in my hand, examining it, flicking through the pages and even smelling it! I love books. How do you treat books? Do you buy or borrow them? Do you religiously return them when you do borrow them? (Book Thief?) Do you treat them with reverence, taking care not to mark them or to turn the page corners? Perhaps each year you put on your white caretakers gloves and take each book down from its designated place on the special shelf so you can iron the pages?

I was like this (except for the ironing) until it suddenly dawned on me one day these were *my* books and I bought them because they had some information in them that I wanted to extract and retain. I deduced that there were two ways to do this, either record it all again somewhere else, which seemed counterproductive or use a highlighter to mark the best lines, paragraphs and links in the book so that it was easy to refer to again when needed. I realise that some people might think this is sacrilege, but don't worry you can get professional help to get past that. Please feel free to try it with this book, I promise I won't be upset. Get one from your drawer now. I prefer to use a bright yellow marker as it looks like sunshine.

The Incidental Landlord

Stumbling outside of my comfort zone

His arms were shorter than mine so his clawing fingers couldn't quite reach my face. I kept my hand firmly on his head as he wriggled and swung his stumpy arms at me. I didn't want to hurt him but equally I really didn't feel the need to test my own pain threshold at that moment in time! I had only been a landlord for 7 months and I had already dealt with much worse than this. The odd thing was I didn't feel at all phased by what was happening; on the contrary I was in fact feeling quite calm. This was becoming the norm and although *'he'* surprised me, the incident itself did not! I actually found it mildly amusing, as I do most things in life. (I often feel like I'm watching my own little life scenarios as they untangle in front of my eyes!). This was to be all part of the so called *'Property Journey'* that every landlord will tell you about. When you deal with property, there is no escaping the people that inevitably come with it, and over the course of my first 24 months of absolute mayhem as a rookie landlord, I found most of these human beings to be extremely unpredictable. My antagonist was rapidly adjusting the trajectory of his haymaker swings so I needed to make a decision and fast!

We are all on a journey from the day we are born until the day we die (and maybe thereafter?) The great thing is that *YOU* get to choose your own Journey. What you do, where you live, how you live, who your friends are - it is all *YOUR* choice. If you are in any way dissatisfied with your life, your income, how you spend your time, who with, how often and where you holiday, you can change it! It took me many years to realise this. Why? Because I, like most people was completely oblivious that there was any other way of life than the one I was living. My life was *'my life'*, if you know what I mean? I was in the Goldfish bowl. It was only when I began to understand there were more choices that my eyes were open to a whole new world of opportunity.

If you are like me, when doors start opening you are compelled to keep moving forward and looking for new doors. When I decided to change the direction of my life, I did this with great enthusiasm and what I discovered enabled me to go from wage slave to financial independence in just 2 short years, the by-product of which is a much more enjoyable life. I've been outside my comfort zone for so long I wouldn't recognise it now if I saw it. It's been interesting, at times extremely challenging but predominately an exhilarating and exciting journey, and I feel I am just at the beginning. Am I special? Not in the slightest, I just made a decision, started on the path and made sure I did something every day to keep me moving along. It's the small decisions you make each and every day that can take you from a mediocre or good life to a great life. It's your choice.

A decision I made was to get some professional property investor training and when I signed up for my first property training session, my vision was that it would be really cool to buy a few more properties over the coming years. That was it! The blinkers were on and that's all I could see ahead of me. It is now almost 3 years later and my portfolio is 20 properties, either owned or controlled (see the Multi-Let section) by myself, my wife Jane and children James and Emily. But what we really couldn't foresee is that Emily and I would become the most results based and sought after Rent 2 Rent (explained later) trainers in the property industry today. We are the trainers that other trainers seek out. We have spoken to over 2,000 people and personally trained hundreds of people, helping them to break the old rules of investing and to *'Turbo Charge their Cashflow'* using our 'Multi-Let Cashflow System' (MLCS), sometimes in just a matter of months. We have also built a brilliant MLCS community (tribe) and best of all is that we have helped so many people escape the life that they were once trapped in (as I was), and we love it! I'd like to tell you how I did it.

But First, Briefly

... the poor Oirish tinkers

Imagine being in your early twenties with a young child, no money, no work and a bleak looking future. This was the situation my parents found themselves in and it forced them into a decision to move away from their family, their friends and their home on the outskirts of Galway in Ireland and to start a new life in the UK. So my sister Maureen was born in Limerick, my brother Tony just made it to English soil and I came along a year or so later. My dad bought a caravan, rented a space on a farm in Somerset, and that's where we all grew up. It was brilliant! A few times during my school years I was stigmatised as being from a family of *'Poor Oirish Tinkers'* - I didn't understand it, I really didn't. Or I had Rhino thick skin even back in those days!

We had a brilliant time growing up on the farm and we had everything we wanted. No TV, no computers, no phones - but we did have a communal bike, an abundance of trees to climb, tractors to sit on, hay-bale dens to make and plenty of trouble to get ourselves into. As kids Tony and I had a great game - we would sneak up on sheep (Steady, I know what you're thinking!) while they slept, jump on their backs and then see who could hold on the longest. It was paradise, I genuinely didn't get it when other kids tried to make fun of my life and I suppose that took their power away, so it stopped pretty quickly. The truth was I actually felt a little sad for them! My sister's favourite trick was hypnotising chickens which she would do by holding them under her arm and stroking their heads and beaks for a while. She then placed them gently back on the ground where they would stand very still for a while and then fall about all over the place when they attempted to walk away. As kids we found this to be tearfully hilarious fun and the chickens seem to quite like it as well.

There were 6 other kids in and around the farm and I couldn't wait to get home every day after school for another mini adventure. The farmer was a lovely old gentleman who (according to my mum) once insisted that accepting the puppy that was leftover from the farm dogs latest litter formed part of our (non-existent) tenancy agreement - he preferred this to drowning it. We jumped up and down with joy at the thought of sharing the already cramped living space with this four legged critter, while my dad mumbled with resignation about 'another mouth to feed' and agreed on condition we christened him Rover. Farms can be dangerous places for little boys to live and I vividly remember twice being bundled into the back of a car and rushed off to hospital. I survived more or less unscathed but thinking back the health and safety brigade would have had a field day as small children and farm machinery are probably a bad mix.

I also have a lingering and somewhat disturbing memory of orange nylon bed sheets and matching nylon pyjamas, which caused huge problems with static electricity in and around the caravan and resulted in me constantly ending up in a heap on the floor whenever I tried to leap into bed! Nevertheless, at aged 8, I was actually very upset with my dad the day he told us we had to leave the farm and move to an official static home (caravan) site several miles away with a much larger 'mobile home' (caravan). When I was 14 he managed to find us a 3 bedroom council house to move into. We were never sure how he managed to do this as the waiting list at that time was as long as the hokey cokey, but I do recall the council official with his clipboard having an Irish accent. Maybe that helped! On a plus side this would at last mean a fridge, an inside toilet and not getting woken up by seagulls tap dancing at 5 a.m. on the caravan roof anymore. On the other hand we would now have to negotiate stairs every morning and evening.

It's all about perspective. I believe everything is about perspective! For my parents, a move to a council house was a major step-up in life. My mum and dad worked very hard to make the house a home; we were given pocket money but we had to earn it and I did a paper round before school, then two. I tried to do three rounds but kept missing the school bus and then had to cycle like a bat out of hell to make it by the end of morning assembly as staying at home was not an option. So I was working hard but not smart at that time - in hindsight I should have employed some younger lads and become their delivery manager! Even in those days I got bored easily and so always worked in the school holidays on one farm or another picking fruit or vegetables out in the sunshine to make some extra money. I would then happily hand the money over to my mum (no Play Station 4 to buy in those days) and go and find some trees to climb with my mates.

Foolproof Top Secret Luck Formula!

with a limited time sensitive offer!

Time can go past slowly or years can pass in the blink of an eye, and a few years later I was married to my beautiful wife Jane with two smart kids, James and Emily. Jane and I had bought a cottage in Bridgwater in Somerset (for the full asking price - doh!) where we had lived for a number of years but James and Emily were growing up fast and the house was becoming too small for our needs. The problem was we had grown emotionally attached to it. We had put our heart and soul into making this a unique cottage with lots of stained glass, reclaimed church timbers and flagstone flooring. We also had many great memories and so deep down we really didn't want to sell it. Maybe next year ...

Another reason we decided it was time to move on from our first house was that we felt our neighbourhood was slowly taking a turn for the worse, since a housing estate was built on fields next to our lovely little cottage. It is human nature to always take the path of least resistance and our lovely little lane that used to open up to fields and horses was now a rat run for the local night clubbers who thought the world needed to hear what they had to say at 3 in the morning. It was turning into a part of town where if they couldn't smoke it, drink it or inject it, they'd torch it!

It was definitely time to pull up anchor and we decided to start house hunting the following year.

Here is the weird bit, the bit where my mother was always convinced that we had a guiding hand from 'up above' (*"It's your Uncle John!"*). We had a dog called Leroy; he was a cross between a retriever and a collie that I had bought for a fiver from a local farmer the year before. This was after 6 months of pleading from the ladies of the house and me putting my foot down and asserting my authority! We took him for long walks at least once a day across the nearby fields. One hot lazy Saturday Jane and I decided to take Leroy for a walk to the town centre, something we had never done before. Jane wanted to buy a few things from the health food store and since I had Leroy with me I waited outside. My attention drifted and I wandered over to a nearby estate agent. When Jane returned I pointed out a lovely big old house in a village where she had grown up. She knew the house and said it was enormous and used to belong to her old science teacher. It was a beautiful natural stone built property looking like it needed some TLC.

On the spur of the moment we went in and asked for the details. The agent asked if we wanted to view it, there was an element of desperation in his voice. We said 'yeah, why not'! The agent was so fed up with driving the 9 miles to show the property to 'tyre kickers', that he didn't accompany us to the property, he just gave us the keys at 4pm that Saturday afternoon and told us to return them on the Monday. We had never met before and he was taking a risk, but I guess we looked like a safe bet. It must have been Leroy the family dog that swung it.

We collected James and Emily (aged 9 and 10) from their friend's house and drove out to see the property. It was thundery weather and started raining - that light misty rain that dries as soon as it hits you. We walked through a big wooden gate to the back of the property. We were hardly speaking; breathing lightly and we were all falling in love with this beautiful old stone building. Before we went in we stood under an ancient Irish Yew tree in the garden, partly to shelter from the now heavier rain but also to fully absorb every second before we turned the key. We had already decided we wanted to live here without anyone saying the words. When we got inside the soot blackened walls indicated there had been a fire, there were mushrooms growing in some of the rooms, nicely propagated whenever it rained by the numerous holes in the roof and the many broken windows. It was a big house and it needed a complete renovation = a lot of work and a lot of money. We decided that we were going to buy it but we had no idea how as we had no money, but that didn't really matter. I find that whenever I have made my mind up to do something the 'how' usually shows up later!

The agent had said it was cash buyers only - I assured him this was no problem (eek!) This meant he would hold the property for us, as I thrashed around desperately trying to find the finance. This took quite some time as I had no idea what I was doing! Which do you do first, find the property or find the finance? The answer is do both at the same time. If the deal is good enough the finance will show up and vice versa.

This property had been at auction twice and not sold. It was in Somerset, the auctions were held in Plymouth, which explains it! The guide price was £100k and the agent indicated that the bank would want 'a little more'! We fell head over heels in love with the place but decided to play it cool and wear our poker faces when we visited the agent to put our offer in. We agreed we were going to offer him £80K and felt a bit nervous about doing this as we had only ever bought one other house before and that was at the

21

asking price. We parked the car and as we walked to the agency I said to Jane 'We can't afford to pay £80k, it will have to be much less. It would have to be £60k!' I estimated it would take £75k worth of materials to get the property up to a basic standard. We were getting close to the shop now and didn't want the agent to see us dithering outside so we continued marching confidently forward. As I swung open the estate agents door, Jane put her hand on my shoulder and smiled, I thought she was going to wish me luck. But the sweet soft voice I had become so accustomed to was replaced by a slow, low almost animal sound - a guttural command, the like of which I have never heard before or since. It scared me. She said *'offer him forty thousand!'*

What!! It was too late, we were inside the agency shaking hands with the happy smiling agent. He could sense that we were not just tyre-kickers and his major problem would soon be fixed. Jane was relaxed while I was breaking out into a cold sweat, as there was now a lot riding on this - James and Emily had already chosen their bedroom paint! After the niceties were out of the way he asked me what my offer was. Without pause and with a steely look that Clint Eastwood would have been proud of, I said forty thousand pounds! From the look the agent gave me you would have thought he just caught me snogging his Grandmother! I countered with my prepared speech about the state of the property and the cost of builders today, blah blah blah. He kept his dead pan gaze on me as he called the bank with the offer.

Jane and I wandered around the office feigning interest in other properties whilst straining to hear the call. Thirty seconds later he put the phone down and with a look that was a cross between disgust, shock and relief he said the property was ours! We saved our celebrations until we were out of sight of the agent and those celebrations slowly turned into mild panic (the strangest mix!)... Where will we get the money? But we *did* find the money and renovated the property to a very high standard over the next 5 years. I find that sometimes the best way to get things done is to create a problem that you must then fix, this really helps you focus.

Many years later, when I was doing my first property investment training course, there was a section on the second day I really liked called the 'Black Ops'. (We have a Black Ops section on our MLCS training now - I'll explain later). I was smiling to myself when the 'questionable' methods for securing a property were laid out for us, as I had applied them myself years earlier when buying this our second property. As soon as our offer was accepted, I drove back to the property and removed any evidence of the 'For Sale' signs and put up a 'Sold' sign I had 'borrowed' after dark from a property in the next town. I also removed the repossession notice in the window. I knew how slippery some banks could be and I didn't want anyone else viewing the property and making a higher offer!

Four years after the work was completed we sold the property for £320,000.

Oh, my secret luck formula is:
Opportunity + Preparation (+ Risk + Bloody Hard Work) = Luck

When Worlds Collide

Living in a Multi-Let

So what happened to that little cottage we were loath to sell? We kept it! The mortgage was down to £4k as we thought it was a good idea to pay it off in those days (Doh!) and so we added it to the mortgage on the new property. Attached to the side of the cottage was a fairly spacious and odd shaped garage which I had been slowly converting into living accommodation and this now had two nice rooms to let. I phoned the local college who supplied us with 2 students, Hannah and Stefan. We agreed a six month let as this was about the time I thought it would take to make part of the new house habitable and enable us to move in. This was our first venture into house sharing and we quickly realised that sharing our kitchen and bathroom with two people we did not know was less than ideal, but we persevered as we were making a much needed £500 per month. They went home between terms and stayed in their rooms most other times, so it was not too intrusive.

Within 24 hours of meeting it became evident that Hannah and Stefan would never become best buddies! He was an Austrian, very organised and travelled, efficient and tidy with a well-rounded view of the world. She was vivacious, loud, very untidy and could easily have starred in an episode of *My Big Fat Gypsy Wedding!* This created a certain amount of tension whenever they were together which was compounded when he overheard her refer to him as 'the rigor mortis man' and suggested he should pay a visit to a taxidermist! It was true that there was something mildly robotic about the way he moved and spoke but nevertheless I still thought that was rather harsh of Hannah! He in turn said she was *a gobby trollop of an English girl'*. Although they went to the same college and left at the same time each morning they never shared a lift in six months. A lesson for later on - make sure as far as possible that house-mates are compatible. Their six tense and awkward months with us came and went with little incident and I decided that before I rented the rooms again I would add a small kitchen and a shower room to make it totally independent. We moved into our new house which meant we could now rent the main cottage for the going rate of £400 per month. It had 2 bedrooms, a bathroom, a big kitchen, sitting room, conservatory and a long garden and was the perfect rental property for the area - we still have it and have never had a problem letting it.

Sharing your living space with strangers who may not have the same ethics or values as you is not something most people do by choice, it is usually due to financial restraints. At the initial happy meeting both sides often fail to mention that they will both have to make many allowances, turn many a blind eye and learn to be extremely tolerant of each other. We have 4 basic rules; don't be noisy, keep the place clean and tidy, pay the rent on time and have a mutual respect for each other. Simple.

MAYHEM

A Baptism of Fire

Welcome to my world

Dictionary definition: any severe ordeal that tests one's endurance - that sounds about right. Emptying a property of all your possessions, taking down all the children's artwork masterpieces and putting them into storage is always going to be tough but we had our sights set on the next property. I had advertised for a tenant in the local paper and agreed the let within days. My referencing process at that time went like this. 'Do you want to rent the house?' 'Yes'. 'OK then, here's the keys'. Simple. You have to understand that I knew nothing about renting a property; I was unaware of any other landlords or trade magazines. I thought that AST stood for Alaskan State Trooper! (I later discovered it was Assured Shorthold Tenancy - a simple contract to use with tenants). My tenant was Sally, a local 40 year old factory worker with a brand new 30 year old, slightly twitchy, boyfriend. She had 4 kids, all different dads; none of them were the boyfriends. All perfectly acceptable as this was what has become affectionately known as NFB (normal for Bridgwater). All went well till week three, when the boyfriend hanged himself.

It happened in the early hours of a Sunday morning and he chose my well-constructed pergola as his 'scaffold'. This I discovered when I went to the house at 9am on the same Sunday to confront them over a bounced cheque.

29

(Yes, he persuaded me to accept a post-dated cheque when he moved in!) When I knocked on the door it was answered by a burly policeman who was at least 6ft 6" tall. He instantly demanded to know who I was! The sad tale of the boyfriend's demise was rolled out by the nonchalant officer.

It eventually came to light that the boyfriend had stolen a chequebook from the girlfriend's dad and had been bouncing cheques all over the place, and now it was all beginning to catch up with him. In the meantime he had been attempting to make a career out of selling hanging baskets that he had been stealing from all over the vicinity in the dark of the night. His get-away vehicle had been a bicycle. He spent the earlier part of his last evening on the planet drinking the best part of a bottle of Vodka after having a major bust-up with the girlfriend.

When the story hit the local press, some my friends were jumping up and down slapping their thighs saying 'I told you so' and advising me, some almost insisting, that I sell the house. I later knew this was known as 'Crabs in a barrel' syndrome. A bucket full of captured crabs will pull down any crab that tries to escape to freedom, in the same way that some people don't like their friends to change as it forces them to question their own life. But I knew this was a one-in-a-million occurrence and was determined to make a success of being a landlord. Little did I know that this was far from my last intervention with the police at this and other properties! My tenant said she didn't want to stay at the property and in the circumstances I agreed. I didn't need to release her from the contract as we didn't have one!

Another Source of Income

Warp speed ahead!

The conversion of the garage into a one bed flat was now complete with a bedroom, a sitting room, shower room, small kitchen and a shared hall. It also had a huge amount of insulation in the walls and ceiling and was a really snug little flat suitable for one person. I placed an ad in the local press and rented to the first applicant, Dave for £303 per month. So together with the cottage it was producing £703 a month. You might have thought the penny would have dropped that this property investing malarkey was the way to go ... but no, I slogged on with the day job for many more years.

Dave was a fully paid up member of the thinking intolerant and had recently become single again when he 'dumped' his girlfriend for refusing to nibble his ears! (I can never understand why some people insist on sharing intimate personal details with strangers?) Dave explained that he had been attacked by a large dog, named Kong, a few years earlier. Part of the process of repair was to graft some skin from Dave's left buttock onto his earlobe. On discovering this, the girlfriends habit of nibbling on Dave's ears suddenly stopped overnight, must to Dave's chagrin.

Dave was a good tenant, kept the place tidy - he had all his *Star Trek* figurines displayed in a perfect line and his *Star Trek* pyjamas neatly folded on the bed. Great, but Dave did have one flaw - he only paid the rent when he felt like it, and with so much *Star Trek* paraphernalia now readily available on the internet, rent was never foremost on his mind. Dave and I entered into a game of cat and mouse. Whenever Dave was late with the rent, I did what I thought every self-respecting landlord did. I changed the lock! Shock horror! I later realised that you were not allowed to do this but at the time it worked very well for us.

So this is how it panned out for the 9 months of Dave's tenancy; Dave's late with rent, I drive to property and change locks. Dave calls me and I meet him at property. Dave pays me and I swap locks back. There was never any animosity or a cross word between Dave and I, just an air of resignation on both sides. When I fondly look back now, the word I think of is 'Bizarre'! I was however somewhat annoyed with Dave when he upped and left in the middle of the night owing me a few weeks rent (I had allowed him to use his deposit to catch up on rent - doh!). Dave left a lot of possessions behind including all his *Star Trek* figurines, his *Star Trek* DVD box sets and his *Star Trek* pyjamas. (I later found out he had a new girlfriend and so assumed he wanted to project a more mature image).

Late the following Sunday evening I found myself loading up my Transit van with all Dave's possessions. This was most inconvenient, as I had a busy week ahead and the local recycling centre (or the Tip as it was then known) was closed. I made a quick decision to return Dave's possessions - as he had obviously just forgotten them. I didn't have his forwarding address but I did know where he worked. It was an engineering company on a nearby industrial estate surrounded by tall metal railing and big metal gates. I drove around for ten minutes until I found it and then stopped the van and piled all Dave's stuff up in front of the gates and finished it off with a nice wooden sign saying 'Possessions of Dave ###'. He had confided in me that he had a problem with timekeeping so I guessed his boss would kindly move his possessions inside when he arrived there at 6 a.m. on that frosty Monday morning. I was just very happy indeed to be able to help Dave in this way!

Delusions of Grandeur

... and police and ambulances

By this time I thought I'd better get a contract for the tenants to sign (this was taking up my valuable time), so I bought a few ASTs from W.H. Smiths on the way to meet Alex and Suzie. They seemed pretty 'normal' (whatever that is) people and promised to look after the house. (I didn't mention the demise of the previous tenants, but the neighbours told them soon enough). A few days after they move in I stopped by to see them. After half an hour I still considered Suzie to be 'normal' but was having serious doubts about Alex's mental health. He was tall and liked to dominate the conversation with his superior knowledge. Suzie was more middle to working class roots, was totally besotted with him and consequently hung on his every word. Alex's nose seemed to be perpetually pointed towards the ceiling and he was so posh that his upper lip never moved when he spoke.

He was in fact the epitome of a Stephen Fry'esque public schoolboy, which was confirmed when he flashed the huge gold ring he was wearing and proudly stated it bore the family coat of arms! 'Oh how interesting' I foolishly replied. Alex mistook my politeness for interest and whipped out a huge chart of the family tree to prove that he did in fact descend from Robin of Loxley!! He then showed me his full size Olympic bow and explained that his huge goal in life was to represent England in the next

Olympics. I was squirming and looking at the door while Suzie looked embarrassed and avoided eye contact by taking a sudden interest in the Laura Ashley wallpaper. (I suspect she had heard this mini rant a few times before). I find it is quite common in life for people to covet delusions of grandeur in an attempt to make them feel a lot better about themselves!

> **Genealogy:** *I have a friend who once paid a genealogist £400 to dig up some information about his family for a book and then another £400 for him to keep his mouth shut!*

Alex and Suzie's 6 months at the property went by without incident until the last week, when the neighbour called me to tell me what Alex had been up to, and report some damage to the property. I also received an early morning call from the police.

Alex needed to get in as much practice as possible and had set up a target, or 'Boss' as it's known in the archery world, at the end of the garden. To get the full range he had paced up the long garden, across the communal path, through the conservatory, through the dining room and into the kitchen. This is where he drew back his massive bow and released arrows at the speed of light. To make it safe for anyone thinking of crossing the communal path he put out 2 small red and white cones! I would probably have never known if not for the fact that in the last month of his tenancy the back door blew shut just as he released an arrow and took out my lovely stained glass window. Alex eventually conceded that a Sellotape repair job was not really sufficient, that the £300 I quoted was reasonable and coughed up. Next time we would take a deposit. We were getting good at this 'landlord' stuff! Alex and Suzie split up when they left my property, Suzie said he was completely wrapped up in himself, and as we all know, people wrapped up in themselves usually make very small packages.

Alex said he had converted the small room into an office. Once when I called at the property to mend the shower I noticed this room now contained a big heavy homemade railway sleeper throne (looked like a school project) and a rather large mirror. I surmised that this was where Alex spent the bulk of his time!

The first attempted suicide: During Alex's tenancy his younger brother came to stay, with his new bride. I later found out this was a marriage of convenience to enable her to stay in the UK. Over the month that they spent together at the property (free of charge!) she fell in love with him, but sadly it was unrequited love. Their relationship fell apart and he asked her to leave and also filed for a divorce. She took an overdose in the early hours of the morning and police and ambulances were called, along with the landlord - me! I recognised some of the officers as they looked me up and down with suspicion. I reassured them I was a nice person by offering them mugs of Alex's coffee. I didn't understand why I needed to be there but they assured me it was standard procedure. Oh the joys of being a landlord!

Peruvian Rain Sticks

... and Llama wool jumpers

This was a sad 3 months. Liz was a calm, slim, lovely and gentle person with long blond hair, bright blue eyes and a permanent tan. She would call me as often as once a week on the premise of needing a small maintenance issue to be done but would soon dismiss it as unimportant and proceed to push her small clothes importing business. She had ethnic clothes and various nik-naks sent over from Peru and sold them from home. Whenever I was reluctant to buy anything she would share her concern at not being able to pay the rent this month and hit me with probably the strangest sales patter of all time. I still remember one particular line; "well someone took half a cup of sweet sassy molassy this morning didn't they?" Huh? She was so sweet ('scuse the pun) that I found myself buying items I didn't need so that she could afford to pay me the rent. How did that happen?

Amongst the many things she persuaded me to purchase, were a very useful rain-stick and an oversized multi-coloured Peruvian real Llama wool jumper with a picture of a pyramid on the back which was obviously designed for a monkey. Her long-time boyfriend was also a nice guy but it was clear from the outside that their relationship was breaking down. He confided in me that he wanted to start a family and to create a normal home with all the usual 'stuff' you find in a family home. I found

37

myself wishing they would talk to each other more often. (I often seemed to adopt the role of 'agony-uncle' with a lot of my tenants). She confided that she wanted to continue with the travelling they had been doing for the last 5 years and that the burden of all their possessions weighed heavy on her. At that time the property had little more than 2 backpacks, a mattress, a table and 2 chairs! (Plus 17 rain-sticks and 30 Peruvian llama wool jumpers). She took minimalism to a whole new level. She wanted fewer possessions and to live a more 'pure' life, he wanted more possessions, including a baby or two, and so even though they were obviously very much in love they went their separate ways. Sad. I still have the rain-stick.

Rubber Bullets

... Playing the system

Michael was a big Irish man with a big voice and, as I was later to witness, a pathologically impatient driver who's hand was either on the horn or hovering over it. He was the other side of sixty and had just separated from his long term partner (this, as it turned out, was a regular occurrence). We had a rule that our tenants must be in full time employment and Michael assured me that he was. Soon after he moved in Michael called me to say he had just been laid off and would be claiming benefits. I soon discovered that he had been without a job for a considerable length of time, was suffering from long term depression and didn't much like to be on his own. So you would have thought that moving into a one bed flat in a different town would not have been high on his wish list! We now have systems in place to check that potential tenants are who they say they are and are also in full time employment, but back in those days we just trusted people to tell the truth. Doh!

Michael would call me at all times of the night and day (once at 2 a.m.) insisting that I came around to talk about the problems at the flat. There were no problems, he just wanted a chat! I had a strict rule of no pets and the first few times I saw his ancient and mingy dog he insisted he was dog-sitting for his brother who had just popped into town for a haircut. Michael was another of those people who thought paying the rent was optional. He was up he was down he was all over the place, his life was a shambles and he did his level best to involve everyone in the clean-up operation.

Towards the end of his tenancy he started to answer the door to people in his grubby Y-fronts and heavily stained string vest. The neighbours were complaining so Jane and I stopped in to see him on the way home only to be told to 'wait just a minute'! I later discovered this was to give him time to shove the elderly dog into the wardrobe! It was nearly dead the poor thing!

On this occasion Michael was fully dressed and was excited to see Jane - he was obviously once a silver tongued lady's man before his poor diet had expanded his waistline to extreme proportions! He handed Jane what I knew to be a large black rubber bullet, a souvenir from the troubles and his days as a young man in Belfast. Jane was aghast and froze as she held it. Michael asked if she knew what it was. I could tell she thought it was a marital aid! Time stood still. She dropped it! I picked it up and enquired if someone shot it at him. Jane looked flustered and confused. Michael promised to pay the outstanding £160 rent and we left. Two days later Michael also left still owing us the money. I had a deposit of £300 and agreed to meet Michael a week later to give him the difference of £140. He had left the flat in a complete mess that took Jane and I six hours to clean up (yes we did our own cleaning back then!). I had been very good to Michael and was annoyed at the state of the flat so I decided I was not going to make things easy for him. When we met I asked for his forwarding address to send the cheque on to, knowing that he would never give it to me. He demanded I pay in cash and started to rant and rave and stamp his feet and threaten me with the best solicitor in town. Eek!

Over the next three months I received 7 or 8 letters from his solicitors, all funded of course by Michael. The solicitor said Michael had driven the 10 miles to his office several times. Ha! I decided to settle the day before it went to court. I dropped off a cheque for £139 - still a pound short just to enrage Michael further. I later found a letter with his new address and so hand delivered a bundle of overdue bills to him with a wink. He was not pleased to see me!

Robert De Niro

... Gone with the wind

The next occupant of the little flat was Dave the taxi driver. When I first met Dave he was upbeat and chirpy and the fact that he offered me free taxi rides clinched the tenancy. He was a big Robert De Niro fan and said he decided on his chosen career after watching the De Niro classic *Taxi Driver*. (I am not making this up!). He was coughing a lot when we met which he put down to the tail end of a severe case of man-flu. Sounded serious! As usual I made an excuse to stop in to check up on the flat a week after he had moved in. Dave's cough was much worse - while I was there he must have coughed up everything except his kidneys! Gross! Dave's mood had also changed somewhat. The chirpiness had been replaced with a permanent look of dark foreboding, accompanied by a face like a bag of spanners. He seemed to resent me being there. Was this the same person I had rented the flat to?

Any time I saw Dave after that and made the mistake of asking how he was, he would list all his woes, who was to blame for them and actually name and count on his fingers all the people that had ever crossed him (he could only ever manage ten, unless of course he took his shoes off and started using his toes as well). I wondered when I would be added to this list. He would then begin a slow and detailed rant of irrational revenge fantasies, possibly taken from an early De Niro movie. Dave also fancied himself as an amateur sleuth and had one of the old CB radios which could tune into the local Police radios. This meant Dave could get to the potential crime scenes fast and he was always on the brink of solving a local crime or one from last week's Crime-stoppers and would therefore soon be claiming the large reward. I thought he would probably be sharing it with his mate Walter Mitty.

I found it quite odd to discover that Dave had a cleaner - it was after all a small flat. I surmised that this was Dave's desperate attempt to get a woman into his bedroom. A few months later the guy next door called me to say Dave had not been back for some time. I called Dave. No answer. Later in the day I borrowed a phone and called him again, he answered. He told me he had to move to London with his job! (Bearing in mind he was a taxi driver!) 'What about your stuff' I asked. 'Oh there's not much there - you can keep it!' Oh that's just great, more junk for me to clear!

I was working locally and an hour later from my scaffolding I saw Dave drive past in his taxi! I tried to contact Dave a few more times to no avail and so decided to clear the flat. We found all his designer clothes (mostly Primark), all his De Niro DVDs, CDs, a stereo, TV, food (mostly pizzas), a brand new leather massaging lazy boy chair with a built in mini beer fridge in the arms and most bizarrely his 'tips' jar containing £178! I later found out he had ran off with his cleaner and now her husband was gunning for him, so Dave was scared to return to the flat in case the ex was staking it out. I think he had been watching too many Robert De Niro movies! Incidentally, I once met his cleaner and thought it was his Gran!

The Shortest Tenancy Ever!

Porn on a Sunday afternoon

The flat became empty *again* and was beginning to be a real drain on my time. I wanted to fill it ASAP, so I accepted the first guy that called (!) I don't clearly remember what Paul looked like because he never looked up - he had a long black greasy fringe, big black rimmed glasses and was always looking to the left and right and at the floor. He mumbled a lot and dribbled a little bit as well - which I assumed was due to an over active saliva gland. We all dribble from time to time, don't we? Paul was one of those people who moved his lips when he was reading.

On top of all this, Paul's personal hygiene standards were somewhat questionable.

He answered the advert, confirmed that he worked full time (a new criteria we had introduced!) and sounded 'OK' on the phone. I agreed to help him move his stuff on the following Sunday afternoon as he didn't have any transport. He lived in a room on 4th floor over a Sainsbury's store and when I arrived he was already packed with all his possessions shoved into 15 or so black bin bags. He opened up one of the bags and pulled out a wad of money to pay the deposit and the rent! It was marked MB for Money Bag! Bizarre.

We quickly bundled all his worldly goods into the van and drove the 2 miles to his new home. I was in a real hurry so parked in the street and started swinging his bin bags out of the van. The bags were the really thin type - not very strong at all and unfortunately in my enthusiasm to be on my way, one such overloaded bag split throwing the entire contents flying through the air!

The pavement became awash with around 50 or so well-thumbed porn magazines! It was a really sunny afternoon; everyone was outside, inquisitive kids on bikes, people washing cars or cutting grass, nosey neighbours and we were attracting quite a crowd who suddenly turned into a swarm of leering gargoyles. Paul froze to the spot as the colour drained from his spotty face. He turned and as white as a sheet, ran into the flat and locked himself in the bathroom. I got some gloves from my van and picked up his 'reading material' which I bundled into the flat with the last of his possessions. Paul was obviously mortified and was making that sound that a dog makes just before it throws up.

I shouted to Paul that everything was in and the keys were in the kitchen. He shouted a pained reply 'Yea, thanks, bye!' I dispersed the crowd and chuckled my way home. Later that evening Paul called to say he had moved out again as the flat 'didn't feel right' for him! He said keep the money for my trouble. It seems that Paul spent most of his tenancy in the loo. Here we go again.

I never saw him after that but later found out he was living in a kind of sheltered home for people suffering from mild paranoia! Apparently the bed baths are great! I'd love to be paranoid - to believe that other people are actually thinking about you! But I realised long ago that most people are far too busy thinking about themselves to notice others; realising this was a great liberation. What other people think of us really is none of our business.

The Young Entrepreneur

Working flat out

At this point it seemed like tenants were coming and going faster than bag-boys in a hotel lobby! Amy was a demure young lady in flat shoes, just short of her 18th birthday and so her father and step mother accompanied her when she viewed the flat. It was the first property they had viewed so I was surprised when the stepmom began to gush and insist 'this was the one'! Her dad on the other hand didn't say much and looked somewhat distant. The step-mum couldn't stop pointing out how wonderful the flat and was asked if Amy could move in immediately. Amy didn't say too much either but smiled with an air of resignation and underlying confidence. The evil stepmother was going to have her way and get rid of her and Amy looked sad and happy in equal measures. This was to be Amy's first time away from home and everyone seemed relieved and grateful when I agreed that she could move in the following day. The dad said he had to run to bank to get the money but in a flash the step-mum pulled out a wad of cash, paid the deposit and half of the month's rent in brand new £20 notes and I agreed that Amy could pay the rest the following day. The meeting ended suddenly when the step-mum suddenly developed a volcanic sneezing fit and hurried out the door spluttering something about an allergy to dogs??

46

When I called in to see Amy a few days later I was pleased to find the flat looking homely, neat and tidy, Amy was a well organised young lady. I gave her a lift to the bank to draw out the other half of the rent but Amy didn't quite have enough money and in fact it took a few months before she sorted herself out financially. She assured me it would be OK as she had secured a secretarial job.

Amy's tenancy was uneventful except for one complaint from a neighbour about doors slamming and Amy's surprising request for a pet rat! She didn't argue when I refused, she just politely accepted my decision - had I at last found the perfect tenant? But it was over all too soon when Amy gave notice to leave after only 9 months. (Incidentally most of our Multi-Let tenants stay between 6 and 9 months)

When I met Amy to do the end of tenancy check-out I was not surprised to find the flat was immaculate. Great. I also noticed she had upgraded her phone, her stereo, her TV and was now a very well dressed young lady. Her clothes looked expensive which made her look older and a little more sophisticated. As we were sorting the deposit she mentioned she was buying a flat. I was surprised she had saved the deposit so fast! As cool as a cucumber she pointed out it was not just a deposit - she was buying the flat for cash! As we said our goodbyes I remembered several concerned phone calls from the new and somewhat puritanical neighbour from across the road at the start of her tenancy with regard to the constant stream of gentlemen arriving at her door most nights … and mornings … and the afternoons! At the time I dismissed it and told them I recalled her mentioning something about a home study chiropody course? Whatever she was doing she was obviously a budding entrepreneur and had been working flat-out! Boom Boom!

I squirted some hand sanitizer on my hands and called a local company to have the flat professionally steam cleaned. The same neighbour called me a few days later to say that she had 14 amateur video clips of what she considered to be admissible evidence, and did I want to collect them! I assured her that I did not.

An Enraged Hobbit

and police and ambulances

This was the second attempted suicide. Andy was vertically and intellectually challenged with questionable personal hygiene standards. He was taken out of school, aged 14, by his dad, who was a builder, and had worked long hours for him for the last 10 years for little recompense. Nice dad! He seemed a tidy enough lad with a haircut any GI Joe would be proud of, but was obviously poorly educated and as he had now fallen out with his dad big time he was consequently struggling to find any work. He really seemed to attract bad luck - he was the sort of person who would catch the bouquet at a funeral! I felt sorry for him and wanted to help him.

In hindsight I tried to help Andy too much - I used to be a sucker for a sob story. Now we have a strict 'No Pay No Stay' policy! Quite a few times I took Andy to work with me to pay off some rental arrears. But his heart (or soft brain) was never in gear and he was always more trouble than he was worth. The end came when I called round to the flat early one Friday evening to collect my weekly sob story and 50% of the overdue rent. He pleaded that he was totally skint yet again and would be staying in to watch re-runs of the *X Files!* Boo Hoo. He was a great (but basic) story-teller and I felt sorry for him yet again and gave him a fiver for the electric meter. What a sucker I was!

Lesson learnt: tenants are not your friends. You must be firm but fair. Never employ them or have a relationship with them and adopt a 'No Pay No Stay' attitude from day one. If you do not do this you will be training them to not pay the rent!

It was a hassle (as always) chasing his missing rent especially as he didn't have a mobile phone. I rushed off home as I was out that evening with some mates on a friend's stag night.

We ended up in a seedy late night drinking hole in Bridgwater, and who did I see at the bar barely able to stand and talking on his mobile phone? Mobile phone! You guessed it! Andy was so drunk he didn't care he'd been caught red handed and was too drunk to even think of an excuse! I made a mental note to go around and see him early next afternoon on my way home from work. No good calling in the morning as Andy would be sleeping it off!

I didn't know what a mess Andy's life was in until I got another call from the boys in blue three weeks later, at 3 a.m. asking me to attend an incident at the flat and bring my keys. They wouldn't say more than that and my mind was working overtime as I drove the 9 miles to the property. When I arrived I found 2 police cars (one of the officers remembered my name from last time, great!) and most of Andy's family stood around looking anxious and glaring at me. Funny how landlords are forever seen as the villains. I had found Andy work, lent him money, let him off rent, given him pep talks, and where had the family been these last few months when he really needed help? There was no sign of his dad.

Andy was threatening to hang himself from the Velux window and wouldn't unlock the door. He was talking to his sister through the locked door. The officer said that after he called me he realised Andy had his key in the door so they would have to break the door down! No chance I thought and formulated a quick plan. I asked his sister to distract him by telling him to look at the Velux window to make sure it was not damaged while I gently turned the key through the lock with one of those tiny screwdrivers that you get free with Christmas crackers. When it was lined up and in position I quickly pushed it out with my key and unlocked the door. One of the burly officers threw me a disappointed look as he pushed past me - he was obviously looking forward to kicking in the door. Andy was standing on a chair and started making a high pitched wailing noise. This was his cry for help.

Lucky for Andy he had a great sister who took care of him and helped him back to health. Andy's sister paid me a little rent over the next 3 months and his mum helped out a bit. Andy was a young man and was now totally reliant on anti-depressants, probably for years to come. He was also in dire need of some personal transport and I had an old *Datsun Sunny* knocking about, so I put 4 re-moulds on it, got it through an MOT, signed it over to Andy and he was mobile again. This may seem very generous on my part but my thinking was that I couldn't really evict him or I'd be named as yet another evil landlord in the local press, and if he could get to work I stood more chance of getting my rent. So it was a totally selfish act on my part really.

A few months later he decided to move in with his sister to save some money. I agreed to meet him at the flat to give him his £200 deposit back. I got to the flat early and it was in an OK condition. But as I looked around I noticed that the key for the electric meter was missing, as were all the door handles and the curtain rings. There were lots of little niggly things that would take time for me to replace. He obviously did this to annoy me but didn't have the brain power to think it through. Why did he do it after I had tried to help him? Who knows, I thought maybe he resented paying me rent or perhaps had not been able to forgive me for unlocking the door for the police officer? When he arrived he was on foot and I asked what had happened to the car? Andy's was one of those rare people whose face was a crystal clear indication as to what was going on in his head - you could easily read his thoughts. When I mentioned the car he bared his teeth and made a growling sound. Better not go there I thought.

After a few pleasantries, I asked where the missing items were? 'Up my Nans' he snapped! 'OK' I said. Silence. 'Where's my deposit?' He demanded. I told him it was in my pocket and he could have it back as soon as he returned all the missing items. Silence. Time passed. I heard church bells in the distance. Andy was thinking. Tumbleweed blew past. Andy's face clearly displayed what he was thinking - it was completely blank! Suddenly it changed to concern as he realised he may not be getting his 200 quid back. The concern morphed into distress - he had probably promised that money to his sister! Finally a look of anger spread across his face. Uh-oh I thought - Andy was not a tall guy but he was a rock solid build, like a bull gorilla. I braced myself; I had been studying Tae Kwon Do for six years and was not feeling phased. Andy dropped his shoulder and charged at me head first - I grabbed his head and jumped back to absorb the impact. For the next minute or so (it seemed a lot longer!) we pushed and shoved. I kept my hand firmly on his head while he flailed his short arms around wildly in a vain attempt to make contact. It was like one of those old black and white slapstick movies! Andy was shouting, I was shouting, so it was inevitable that the guy who had just moved into the adjoining cottage would soon appear in the shared hallway, and he did.

Peter was a big man, at least 6ft 3", and had moved in next door less than a week earlier. He viewed the property on his own as his wife Amber was in hospital (this was a partial truth). He could have been a stunt double for John

Merrick (The Elephant Man) and had a voice like Mr Bean, but I didn't hold that against him when he rented the property.

By this time I had Andy held on the floor with my knee on his chest. His short arms were still failing to make contact with me but he was concentrating hard and adjusting the range of his clenched fists. By now I was half laughing and telling him to calm down - which seemed to enrage him even more! Peter was extremely agitated and very upset by what he was witnessing. I had assured him a few days earlier that it was a quiet neighbourhood! I told him to stay calm and call the police. He swiftly wandered back into the house with his mobile phone pressed to his ear, I recall him mumbling in his best Mr Bean voice, 'Heelloo, is that the Police?'

Seconds later Andy had wriggled free, jumped up and darted out the door. By the time I went outside he had already sprinted at full pelt half way up the lane. Usain Bolt couldn't have caught him! I heard some vague threats shouted back over his shoulder but never saw or heard from him again. I shrugged.

Life is 10% how you make it and 90% how you take it for sure. As the late great Jim Rohn once said; "Your personal philosophy is the greatest determining factor in how your life works out."

So back to Peter. What I didn't know when I rented our lovely cottage to Peter was that both he and Amber were convicted sex offenders. Oh Dear oh Lordy!

God Bless You

... and may he come for you soon

How did I come to rent to paedophiles Peter and Amber? Well, I was totally focused on my building company and I was just starting a major new project, so I wanted to rent the property as fast as possible to the first applicant that came along. Peter sure was an odd looking character - God definitely threw away the mould after he made him but I didn't hold that against him as he was very well spoken and well mannered! Peter said Amber was in hospital and this was kind of true. Every time they moved, which was often, she had to go into a respite home as she couldn't cope with the stress. When I say 'moved' they were usually drummed out of town when the neighbours found out what they were!

Peter had responded to my ad within hours of it going live and we agreed the tenancy that same evening. I quickly learned a lesson to never accept the first applicant. Peter wore a good suit and drove a fairly new car. He said that he worked for a local disability company (a lie) and his wife Amber (false name) loved gardening and loved cleaning (more lies). They seemed like the perfect tenants and at last my troubles were over! I congratulated myself on my good selection and relaxed. A few days later a neighbour from across the road called me to say Peter and Amber were on the sex offenders register and if I didn't get them out right

54

away he would burn the house down! Oh dear oh lord, here we go again.

This was a different game we had to play - I didn't want to confront them, what good would that do. I had to be careful not to upset them as they were not stupid and could cause me a whole lot of trouble. On top of all this I had just watched a DVD called *Pacific Heights*. If you are considering renting a property do NOT watch this movie!

So what to do? We went to the police for advice and they said do nothing. Great, that's really helpful! They were very aware of who they were and told us to be very careful as to what we say and do. I asked if they knew the property was within half a mile of a school. Yes they did. I asked if they knew that Peter now had an invalid scooter and would ride it around when the school kicked out with a few balloons tied to the back to attract kids. No they didn't know that but they would look into it, and a week later paid him a visit.

Peter and Amber were not working and blamed ill health. They were very good at working the system and had been doing it for years. They were given a newish car, an invalid scooter (not sure why), had a dog so they could claim more, were given a voice activated computer, furniture, the list goes on and on. I really don't get it. Anyone could see that the both of them were quite capable of working and yet here they were getting handouts for year after year, while I was working hard to pay taxes to support them! Grrr! They were also members of a local church group and often spoke of all the good work they were doing for the community and although there was never any evidence to support it, they supposedly went to church every Sunday.

Personally I think that just standing in a church doesn't make you a good person any more than standing in a garage makes you a car!

55

So we decided to sit it out. The tenancy was for 6 months and I would follow the route I had been advised to take by the National Landlords Association, of which I had recently become a member. I would issue a Section 21 at the relevant time for Peter and Amber to leave and keep our fingers crossed that they would in fact leave, and no damage would be done to our property. I explained this to the neighbours and along with the police we all agreed to monitor them very closely.

So every few weeks I would make an excuse to visit the property to carry out small maintenance issues. One of the first jobs I decided I would do was to tile the small shared hallway. The flat was empty for a few days and there was a back door to the cottage so no problems with an alternative access. I laid all the tiles in a day except for the four ones that went under Peter and Amber's door. Frustrating as it was I had to ask their permission and they were not home so I arranged to do it the next day when they were back.

Amber was a very odd lady. Something I noticed about her early on was that she would always maintain a lower eyelevel than anyone else in the room. Some sort of submissiveness I guessed. So if I was standing she sat and if I sat she knelt on the floor. I arrived at the property, Peter let me in and I started laying the last few tiles under the door. The noise must have woke Amber (it was only 11a.m. after all!) and she came down stairs, made a cup of tea and knelt on the floor to talk to me. I smiled to myself and knelt on the floor as well. Concern flashed across her face and she slid down lower to rest on one elbow. I countered by sliding down to roughly the same level. She glared at me and lay flat out on the floor with her head resting on her hands. As I was tiling a floor I had the perfect excuse to get my eye right down on the floor to check the level without appearing too odd. She was beat. She couldn't get any

56

lower than that! She let out a sound like someone had stepped on one of those squeaky dogs toys, jumped up, and grabbed her tea, spilling it everywhere as she ran back up stairs. She also suggested that I had no parents. She was on to me!

I was just about finished and packed up my tools. When I came back in Amber had obviously been downstairs and stepped all over my tiles! I re-set them and packed up again. When I returned she had done the same thing again. Darn! Once again I re-set them but this time took a deep breath and shouted to Peter in my most authoritative voice - *'Peter! Tell Amber that if she steps on these tiles one more time I will evict you both today!'* 'No problem' he replied. It was just bluff of course but it did the trick.

Years earlier I had built a lovely little brick fireplace with special small reclaimed bricks I had discovered. At around month 3 into the tenancy I called in to do an interim inspection (my first one ever!) to find that Amber had painted the fireplace a bright blue. Argh! She didn't even do a good job as there was more paint on the carpet than the fireplace. I explained that she had broken the terms of the tenancy and it needed to be cleaned off within seven days. She made a grumbling noise from where she was lying on the floor and said she would try. Seven days later I returned to find her attempting to clean a brick and failing spectacularly. I told them both I would be back on the weekend to remove this fireplace and rebuild a new one for which they would have to pay. I was fuming but also found Peter and Amber's reactions strangely comical - him on the sofa, her on the floor and both with mouths wide open - in rehearsed shock. Their whole tenancy was turning into a second rate soap. I noticed more of the same blue paint splashed around here and there but decided to wait till they had vacated to sort it out. What joy!

I never used to let minor stuff like this rattle me - it was only 'stuff' after all, I would just sigh deeply and get on with it. As a landlord you can't allow the actions of your tenants upset you, if you do you will probably be upset most of the time. A problem is only a problem if it is viewed as a problem.

Peter had asked if BT could install a phone line in the shed at the bottom of the garden as he was a keen handyman and would spend a lot of time there. I knew straight away this was a lie as there was never any sign of any tools when he moved in. A week later I visited the property to discover that BT had done a very poor installation, with cables draped over the top of Velux windows so that you couldn't open them! You could train monkeys! I called BT to complain and eventually was transferred from Mumbai to someone in Grimsby. There was confusion as the address was correct and the engineer had definitely been out but the name was different? I instantly realised what Peter was doing - he wanted an internet connection in the shed but didn't want it to be in his name for obvious reasons. I made it clear what his full name was, I slowly spelt it out and got the operative to read it back to me a few times to confirm. I also called the case officer at the police station and filled him in. I waited around to confront him and an hour later Peter came home. I explained what had happened but told him not to worry as BT now had the correct name. I maintained a look of complete innocence. He didn't smile and he didn't thank me!

This unsavoury couple eventually left at 6 months and 1 day. I told them a tale about needing the house back for a family member and was sorry to see them go(!) but I suspect they were already making plans as they probably never stayed anywhere for longer than six months at a time. The last I heard they had moved to the other side of town, half a mile from a school. I rang the case officer and he said they would look into it.

There are lots of things in life that don't make sense to me these days - friendly fire, mandatory options, inheritance tax, an open secret, a holy war, a dry lake, authentic reproductions, a new tradition, silent alarm, limited lifetime guarantee and the term uninvited guest - you can be one but you can't be both! I also don't understand why the police don't take absolute control of situations like this instead of waiting for 'something' to happen, and then responding to it, too late. It makes me want to indulge in an involuntary personal protein spill.

The Heroin Addicts

Francis! You Muppet!

When we had got rid of the last tenants Jane confided in me that she thought I was a complete and utter Muppet and that she could choose a better tenant on a dark night with both eyes closed! My tenant finding confidence was at a particularly low point at that moment in time and so I conceded temporary defeat. I had recently accepted a well-paid short term contract in Nottingham and was away during the week, so Jane arranged to meet her top selection from the eight applicants on the forthcoming Saturday afternoon at 2 p.m. Jane said the young lady had split from her partner and *'just wanted a new start for her baby and her'*. We had all the relevant paperwork and were finally looking forward to a peaceful time with no dramas.

As we drove down the quiet lane I saw a skinny as a stick homeless person standing outside our property beside a beaten up old pushchair. Surely this couldn't be her! We drove slowly closer. As we pulled up I looked into her eyes and she looked into mine. Oh dear. I said out of the side of my mouth 'Jane, you can't be serious; we cannot rent our property to this person', all the while maintaining a fixed smile as I applied the handbrake. Jane of course thought I was just being pedantic until I pointed out that the poor waif was wearing clothes that Oxfam would have refused, had eyes like two pee holes in the snow, teeth like a deserted graveyard and skin the colour of a sun bleached

60

banana. To me this screamed out one word - junkie! There was no way we could rent our house to this person. Jane suddenly saw it and told me to deal with it!!! What a yellow belly! I jumped out of the car wearing my best smile and said, 'Hi, we are so sorry but as we pulled up we realised we have left the front door key at home! Whoops! Can we meet again in the week?' A demonic expression flashed across her face, it was like a still from the Exorcist! We had a brief glimpse of what the future could have been like. She quickly regained her composure and said, 'Sure, no problem'. We were all smiling that weird awkward fake smile that people do.

Someone was shouting in a croaky voice - 'Hey mate, Hey buddy!' 'Over here'! I turned and looked to see a guy that could easily have been her evil twin half way up the lane. He looked like a monkey with arthritis. 'Who's this?' I enquired. She replied 'oh him, that's the baby's dad, I've got a restraining order on him so he's not allowed within 50 yards of me and the sprog!' Oh lovely, that's just great! Talk about a close shave, this would have been such a fun tenancy! As we said out goodbyes, images of the Exorcist and the Omen kept flashing into my head - I was too scared to see what was sat in the pushchair. The thought of it left me blinking for days.

Over the next few days I fielded calls from both the lovely lady and her estranged boyfriend, ranting and raving about how *absolutely dreadfully* they had been treated. I usually slid the phone quietly back into my pocket and let them get on with it whilst running up their mobile phone bill. They eventually hung up after a few minutes and the calls eventually stopped.

With bitter experience we have learned to take a bit more time in choosing our tenants. A quick decision at the start often results in a slow and painful extraction from the property later on. Don't always accept the first person that comes along, even if they are very charming and seem the perfect tenant.

Let's Get Serious

... Claiming our lives back

At this point Jane and I were not having fun; all these tenant issues were taking way too much time and we decided we were going to finally start taking it seriously. Like the proverbial needle in a haystack, we needed to find the perfect tenant but how <u>do</u> you choose the perfect tenant? All these years later I am still not sure. You can thoroughly reference, go on gut feeling, ask to meet the tenant at their existing property, get insurance, ask for guarantors and even then they may turn out to be a lowlife at the end of the tenancy, although to be honest this rarely happens these days. There will always be an element of risk and its all par for the course. All you can do is tick every box to protect yourself as much as possible. The most important thing is not to allow it to stress you out. I have discovered a great way to deal with all this stuff and stay completely calm, which I'll tell you about later.

We sat down and went through the remaining seven applicants on the list. We called them all back and asked for the name and phone numbers of their employers so we can do a reference check. Incredibly we had never done this before and it cut the list down to just three! Some people write down any old rubbish on application forms. When I phoned the Government office where one applicant claimed to be employed I was greeted with a gruff 'Yes mate'. When I told him who I was there was a long pause as he composed himself and then he completely changed his tone and put on his best telephone voice. Too late my son!

One of the applicants had three kids and as it was a two bedroom cottage we thought they wouldn't stay long and dismissed them. So two applications left and one of them was a 22 year old lady and her partner - they both worked, were very polite and we thought we had found the winner, until he casually mentioned he was the drummer in a local band and has a full sized drum kit! As we discounted them I realised this was fun - I felt like Sherlock Holmes. I guess that would make Jane *Miss Marple?* So this meant there was only one suitable applicant really and we called them to see if we could meet at their existing property to check it out. We said we needed to drop some forms around and gave them an hour's notice. Lots of landlords don't like doing this as they feel awkward but to be honest I find it much more awkward when I get a tight-fisted dirty low down non-paying tenant!

The house was spotless; the two young kids were smart and polite. We drank tea from clean mugs (I always hated it as a builder when I was offered tea in a dirty mug - like they thought I was a heathen or something!) The lady willingly showed me her husband's last 3 months bank statements. This is a powerful reference check as it shows that the applicant has a job, can afford the rent, is currently paying the rent and does not overstretch himself each month. After a quick check that his employer's number was kosher and a phone call on the spot to his boss, I whipped out the contracts and we got them all signed up there and then. They had 3 weeks still to run on their tenancy but were so desperate to get away from the area that I agreed to let them move in the next day and when the flat next door eventually became available they rented that too. They have now been with us for 13 years; never missed a payment and the house and garden are looking good.

I get the odd phone call from the guy who always sounds disappointed when I answer - I'm sure he is checking to see if I'm still alive because if I was dead he could stop paying the rent. Is there such a thing as the perfect tenant - time will tell?

The Penny Starts to Drop

... and a brand new lunatic enters the asylum

Remember that old stone house that Jane made me bid £40k for? Well it was a big house - too big for us really. We discovered that it used to belong to the village doctor around the turn of the last century, and he had built a large stone surgery on the end of the property with its own door onto the street. Jane saw this as an elegant music room or a library, whereas I saw it as another and very welcome stream of rental income. The penny was at last beginning to drop and I was really beginning to understand and love the concept of property investing - doing the work once and getting paid for it over and over again and I decided we needed to do much more of this!

So I set about converting this space into a self-contained unit and created a separate shower room by sealing off the connecting doorway into the main property. Due to the thickness of the old stone walls and the dilapidated state of the building, it was a difficult conversion that took 6 months of really hard work at evenings and weekends. I also built a large stone porch to the rear and it used to make me really grind my teeth when people would tell me how 'lucky' I was to have this additional income! I thought of all those winter nights with a wind tearing at the plastic sheet I had rigged up over me to keep the rain off as I worked - luck had nothing to do with it! Grrr.

So now we had a cottage making £400 a month and a flat producing £300 per month that covered our mortgage plus an additional £300 per month from the annexe which covered some of our monthly bills. So did I jump into Property investing full time? Ummm ... no! Although I was starting to 'get it', 'financially free' was still not a phrase I had ever heard and so at that time did not even consider the concept. I had never read the Robert Kiyosaki classic *Rich Dad Poor Dad* or indeed any other educational books. I was running low on capital and at that time had no idea how to raise joint venture finance. Looking back I can see I was living life in semi darkness and it was only on discovering the whole world of adopting the correct mindset, mixing with like-minded people, constantly educating myself and constantly moving forward, that I've felt like the lights are slowly being turned on.

If you are looking for something to while away those endless cold winter nights, a great little investment would be the Cashflow 101 board game which forms a part of the Rich Dad Empire that Robert Kiyosaki has built. It costs circa £60 and is available from Amazon. Playing this game with friends and family is great fun and can be very revealing as to everyone's attitude to investment and risk. It's been described as Monopoly on steroids and is an entrepreneurial education for sure.

The day came to rent out the annexe. We were now seasoned landlords and knew what to expect so nothing would go wrong, right? Well not quite! Katie seemed like a nice lady (they always do at first!), she was a strawberry blond, or was she ginger, I'm not sure? She wore a big flowery dress, jumped around excitedly all over the place and was very bubbly. When I look back I can see that she was trying desperately to keep a lid on her own personal brand of insanity. She moved in and then things changed - the knocking on our door started the very next day - she told me that she didn't trust doorbells! Oh dear. We entered into an uneasy conversation which ended abruptly when I asked her where she was when John Lennon was shot ... she thought I was accusing her!

Complaint number one was the ticking of the electric meter - she insisted it was deafening and wanted something done about it. I said lets go and have a listen. She had flowers and big flowery artwork everywhere and it looked great, but a little voice in my head said 'Artists are unpredictable and temperamental'!

Katie 'ordered' me to come around at 4 p.m. on Saturday afternoon. I complied. She had just brewed some strong coffee and without asking thrust a small bone china cup into my hand. The air was so thick with the pungent smell that it made my eyes water. You could have stood a spoon up in the treacly substance. I knew if I drank it I would not sleep for 3 days and suddenly began to understand the root of the problem as Katie poured herself a second mug! So we stood there in perfect silence straining to hear this accursed ticking. Nothing. After a full minute of us playing statues with odd expressions, I went to speak 'Katie , I ... ' . She shushed me in no uncertain terms, holding up her long piano index playing finger; it was obvious who was in charge here! I shrank back down and waited. Minutes passed. At last she let out a deep breath and relaxed and asked how anyone could be expected to sleep through that! She was now breathing rapidly and deeply with eyes darting all over the place. I had heard nothing, not a tick nor a tock, not even a whisper. I replaced the bone china cup and started slowly backing up and promised to take care of it as I bolted out the door, thankful to be alive.

The following five days brought forth three written complaints shoved through my letterbox at various times of the day about the noisy tractors driving past (we lived in a Somerset village!), the distance to the shop (exactly the same as when she moved in!) the weather (out of my control), the colour of the lampshades (her own), a creaky door etc. Then she want quiet for a few days, which worried me more. I knew that whilst a quiet man is usually a thinking man, a quiet woman is usually hatching a plot! So I put a note back through Katie's door asked if she wanted to be released from the contract and move on. When we all returned from work/school the next day she was gone. She left a load of artwork, some of it good, and said we could keep the money and the art for our trouble. A very odd lady indeed.

The rest of the tenants who stayed in the annexe were disappointingly normal.

A
BIT
MORE
MAYHEM

On the Merry Go Round

is this as good as it gets?

I have always been one of those *busy* types, I get bored easily and am always looking for something to do and ways to make a few extra pounds, and I was the same as a kid. The village where I grew up was a mile away from the main route to the West Country and Cornwall. During the summer the overloaded cars with kids hanging out of them and the towed caravans and motor homes were end to end, but unfortunately these country roads were just not designed for such heavy traffic. This resulted in annual traffic jams with vehicles inching along the hot steaming tarmac.

About two miles from my village was a garage with a good sized shop that sold ice creams. One year aged about 13, I had an idea! I borrowed £10 from my mum along with the small cool-box we had. I chose an accomplice from the village (it's always a good idea to have an accomplice in life in case it all goes wrong so you have someone to blame!) and we went to the garage and bought 20 lolly pops. The owner thought we were a little odd but we were saying nothing until our little business venture was a success. We walked a half mile away from the garage and put up our home made sign - 'Ice Cold Lollies only 50p'! This was actually a 100% mark-up which irritated some of the dads but with the wife and kids howling in their ears how could they refuse.

Two hours later the garage had sold out of every lolly and cold drink in stock and we had made a great wad of cash for us and for the garage owner. Every Friday during the summer we would pray for a weekend scorcher and we repeated the process for a month. The odd thing was that the garage owner didn't seem very happy that we were making money from his stock and after 4 weeks told us we were banned from his shop! What a philistine! There were other shops and we ran this little enterprise for several more summers before we got distracted by schoolgirls. In hindsight we should have played a few shops off against each other for a discounted rate as we were actually in the 'trade' ourselves!

My school years were followed by a squandered year in college where all I left with was a round of applause, and then a variety of jobs in construction before I decided to train as a carpenter. (I figured that if it was good enough for the son of God, it was good enough for me). I then kind of morphed into general building before I had enough of working for other people and started my own small building company, circa 1990. I lived and worked all my life in Somerset. I went through that stage that most people go through - thinking the grass was greener somewhere else, before I realised the grass in Somerset was green enough and it was a beautiful part of England. My parents had chosen well.

Twenty years of gratifying but very hard work followed. I really loved creating and the more challenging the project, the better. I often took on difficult jobs that other guys walked away from. When I think back it was also partly due to getting easily bored and wanting a new challenge. If I liked the customer and the sound of the project, my answer was usually 'yes' before I had fully understood the question! As Richard Branson says 'Screw it, let's do it!' I would then try to get the guys all fired up with my enthusiasm, but unfortunately employees often don't see things in quite the same way as their boss.

> *Top Tips if you employ people:*
>
> *1. When in doubt, mumble.*
> *2. When in trouble, delegate.*
> *3. When in charge, ponder ... it never fails!*

I had a beautiful house, three rental incomes, good vehicles, excellent holidays and a super-duper life. My little building company primarily did high-end loft conversions and renovated big old country houses for C list celebrities, with at one time 17 people working for me on site. It was hectic, all-consuming and fulfilling work. *BUT,* when I couldn't work due to economic or meteorological conditions, I didn't get paid, and Britain is prone to its fair share of both! Looking back I was working very hard indeed.

Around this time my beloved mother became seriously ill. I had big work and huge financial commitments at that time as I had just bought another three story colossal farmhouse, this time together with a massive barn to convert. So I usually only got to see her in the evenings after work and by that time the morphine had kicked in and she was, as she put it, *'away with the fairies'*, and then she died. Boom! I was devastated. What the hell was I doing? The centre of my universe has just been snatched away from me and instead of spending time with her, there I was working for a faceless bank! I suddenly realised I was stuck on life's merry go round, entrenched in the Rat Race. I felt I had no control over my time, my finances or indeed my life and I felt pretty stupid!

Many years earlier, when my dad died from a brain tumour, still a young man in every way, I was working for a local building firm. I wasn't able to take much time off throughout his illness due to low wages, mortgage/bills to pay, the demands of my then employers and the fact we had decided Jane would stay home with James and Emily until they started school. We both knew these formative years were very important for children, but it meant there was little spare money. It filled me with so much regret that I did not spend as much time with my dad as I had wanted to and then it was too late. He was gone. I told myself I would never allow that to happen again. Then I got caught up in my busy-busy-busy life and put it to the back of my mind, and now, 20 years later, I had allowed it to happen all over again with my mum! Was this as good as life was going to get? What did I have to look forward to but another 20 years of hard work? What of my children James and Emily, would they also have the 20 year slog that Jane and I had experienced?

There had to be a better way.

Our First Multi-Let

... and a gift from the Government

I once said in a magazine article that investing in Multi Lets is the 'Lottery winners approach to property investing!' With a single let property you have one stream of income and if the property is empty or the tenant stops paying, you have a problem. With Multi Lets you may have six streams of income landing in your bank account each month and with the exponential growth of this sector, and as long as you have the correct systems in place, you really can't fail.

So how did we come to buy a Multi-Let? Emily had completed her first year of an Architectural Degree at Bristol UWE. She decided that one year in Halls of residence was quite enough and checked out a few local house-shares, which she found to be messy and over-priced. I couldn't believe what we had to pay for the outdated, draughty, noisy, hostel-style room with only space for a single bed that was in dire need of updating and had an idea - I would buy a property near the Uni to convert to a Multi-Let for Emily and 5 other students to live in. A quick calculation meant that we would be making in excess of £1k net per month with Emily living free. There was enough equity in my first Buy to Let to use as a deposit and pay for the refurbishment and so I did what I always do - I took MASSIVE ACTION and spent a few days viewing, making offers, arranging finance and

77

planning. This was 2008, everything was selling fast for over and above the asking price and I needed to get my timing right so that the property was bought and refurbished in time for the next student year - miss it and I risked having an empty property for twelve months. Eek!

Most people like to be a part of something bigger than themselves and so join clubs and organisations throughout their life to find commonalities with other people - we all like to belong. Whenever I am buying a house I try to find the common ground with the property owner - as we know people prefer to do business with people they like. So Emily and I arrived at this property, it was perfect for what we were looking for and we had already been outbid on three previous properties. Time was running out and I was determined to get this one. Emily arranged the viewing and up until this point I have just shaken hands with the agent and said 'Hi'. We ring the doorbell and are greeted by a charming and retired Irish lady. The agent and Emily lead the conversation and there's another 'Hi' from me as I search frantically for a connection ... but nothing was forthcoming.

Emily told the lady she had a lovely accent and asked where she was from. *'Spiddal, just outside Galway'* she said, and asked if we knew it. I don't know what came over me, desperation I suppose, but I found myself answering in a mild Irish accent!!!! Emily gave me a 'what are you doing Dad' look, but it was too late to turn back now, I had to keep ploughing on. Actually it was pretty easy for me as my parents were both from the same area so the accent and pronunciations felt natural for me and I knew the region a little as well. The nice Irish lady and I really gelled and so we left Emily and the agent to get on with the viewing while we babbled away. I let her do most of the talking.

Forty minutes later we left with big smiles all around except Emily who still looked somewhat apprehensive. The agent left and we pulled an old trick by going back to the house twenty minutes later to confirm something we had 'forgotten' - I think it was to ask the make of the boiler or something? This gave us an opportunity to have a nice relaxed chat without the agent being there, we really bonded this time and the lady told us there was another offer but she really wanted us to have the property. She kept her word and our offer was accepted. The agent was a bit miffed that we had returned to the property without him but he soon got over it.

Everything worked like a well-oiled machine. Emily had persuaded 4 of her friends to move in with her - it's amazing how a precise deadline can focus your attention. The planning application for the extension was passed in the shortest possible time. Finance was in place, the building work went smoothly and we finished just in time to catch the student year. I am often told that I am lucky but I am no luckier than anyone else. It's just that most people don't recognise luck when it knocks on their door because it turns up wearing overalls and looks like hard work!

The property was next to the site of a new hospital and housing development that was being built. As the hospital was right behind the property it would change the views from the rear windows and possibly reduce the light. In reality it was far enough away not to matter to me and I had no problems with a nice new hospital being built - there will soon be a good supply of young doctors and nurses for our rooms! So I was somewhat surprised when a gentleman contacted us with regard to paying us some compensation for blocking our views and reducing our light. He suggested £7k!

I think the only people who say 'I don't need the money' are people with no imaginations! I can always find a home for some money. I countered that the huge hospital has reduced the value of my property by at least £15k, and so we settled on £10k, which came in very handy thank you. I never thought I would ever thank Mr Cameron for anything!

The house was finished and ready on time, only went £2k over budget and Emily got to pick the best room. She lived there rent free on the condition that she takes care of the running of the house, which she did for four years. This was great experience for her that would prove to be very useful in a few short years' time and it also allowed me to remain the Incidental Landlord. My estimations were correct and this Multi-Let started generating £1.3k net per month, which added to the £700 we were making from the first property was a very nice monthly income. So did I jump into property investing full time? Umm, no - the penny failed to drop and I slogged on with the day job!

What happened to the other £300 rent from the annexe? We sold this property three years previously and moved 20 miles away into an old farmhouse that needed complete renovation. With the house came a barn with planning permission for a three bed dwelling. The two projects took 18 months of solid work to complete followed straight away by our first Multi-Let project. This was a tough time for me as I developed a back problem which at times rendered me unable to get out of bed in the morning! I desperately wanted to get up and get on with the day but just could not physically manoeuvre my feet to the floor. A by-product of this was severe sleep deprivation and my energy levels hit the floor. All the signs were there to tell me it was time to move on from the construction industry and enter the world of property investing full time.

Out of the Goldfish Bowl

... and into the pool of filth!

Pretty much the day my mum died, my wonderful sister Maureen was diagnosed with terminal cancer and given six years to live. She died suddenly just two years later. Maureen was without doubt the bravest person I have ever had the honour to have known and one of those rare souls capable of unconditional love. Maureen had a particularly nasty strain of cancer which she bore with great dignity and grace. Her heart stopped beating during the operation to remove the tumours and she was put into a coma for a month to allow her to slowly recover. It was a really tough time for all the family as we sat by her bedside holding her hand and talking to her, never really knowing if she would regain consciousness.

As she made a very painful recovery she never once complained and no matter how bad things got for her, her concern was always for others. I really cannot put into words what her loss did to my family and so will not try. But she too was instrumental in knocking me out of the life I had been stuck in for too long and I owe her so much for that. When our mother died, I related my frustrations at feeling trapped in the life I had created for myself and Maureen encouraged me to change, she said 'Francis, you can do anything you put your mind to, just do it'. It was all I needed to hear - that someone who knew me so well had

81

complete faith in me. Some people carry money next to their hearts, I carry a photograph.

So I decided to embark on a completely different path from the one I had been following for the last 20+ years, (Eek!) and I decided to go for total immersion. I have never been one to do things by half and this new 'property investing' life was to be no different. I was warned by friends to 'think again' before entering into that 'pool of filth', but I saw things a different way ... so I held my nose and jumped right in!

Talk about when worlds collide - at that same time I read an article that stopped me in my tracks and made me realise I was well and truly screwed and totally embedded in the rat-race. The article pointed out that if they received no income for 3 months, 'most' people would be in deep financial trouble. I dismissed this as it obviously did not apply to me. But it continued to play on my mind and agitate me. When I got home later that evening I made a big mug of green tea and sat down to figure it out. Pretty soon I realised that I was in fact 'most' people.

I was in shock and felt cheated. I had worked really hard my whole life with barely a day off sick only to realise I had built it all on foundations of dust (another builders analogy!) All that hard work, and for what? Being a builder I also had access to the daily rags and like everyone else was becoming more and more disillusioned at the greed of our bankers, at our disappearing pensions and the behaviour of the members of parliament - our so called elected leaders! I was getting older every day and suddenly my future was starting to look like an episode of Bleak House! I felt a little panic. I thought I'd been doing OK but now realised that it only looked like I was in front because I was so far behind!

I would regularly read the Sunday Times Rich list as I found it interesting to discover how 'the other half' lived and how their fortunes were made. I always had mixed feeling when reading it. I felt riches like that were unobtainable for me but at the same time knew that we were all the same people with the same hours in the day and the same opportunities (Well almost!).

Looking back I guess I was developing a desire for a better life for myself and my family and was looking for clues. The construction industry would hold no surprises for me - it was about as good as it was going to get and It seemed the harder I worked and the more I earned, the more we spent on the money merry-go-round! Around this time I cashed in the joke of a pension that I'd been paying into for years.

'If work was a good thing the rich would have it all and not let you do it!' Rex Harrison

Interesting statistic: *Britain's 5 richest families now own more wealth - £28 Billion - than the poorest 20% of the population! (Oxfam)*

A Fork in the Road

Hesitation will make your doubts come true

Have you ever had that dream where you are running in quicksand and everyone else is speeding past you? When my mum died, I had experienced a significant 'mind shift' - I felt like I'd been running in quicksand for too many years ... I didn't like it and decided I was going to do something about it! It was time to get off the fence and *Take Action!!* I thought I could do more and be more, I felt like I was only running on two cylinders. Do you ever feel like that? Days were beginning to become monotonous for me so it was time for a new challenge (Jane says I was looking for an adventure, to which I replied 'adventures only happen when there is insufficient planning my dear!).

But I desperately wanted to be in control of how I spent my days and who with. But how? What was I going to do? I have always loved everything about property and had for some time been harbouring a secret desire to expand our little property empire, but I had no idea how anyone could buy multiple properties without saving up another huge deposit! I had bought a few property books but needed something more. So I began researching where everyone researches these days - the internet - In fact I turned down a few smaller building jobs to give me some free days to stay home and do solid research. As soon as I started looking I became totally overwhelmed with the amount of information out there as I subscribed to every newsletter and forum going. I discovered a multitude of property investment training companies offering to make me rich ... if I gave them a large chunk of my money. Maybe I was missing something but that didn't really compute with me!

After 4 months of searching and 'registering my interest' with every 'guru' going, I narrowed it down to two companies that I resonated with. One of those companies had an open day in Heathrow coming up and so I booked a place for myself and Jane at £50 each. It was a painful decision for me to part with £100 as I had never paid for any education in my life; it was a totally alien concept. In fact I told Jane it was a free day so that she wouldn't think me a complete idiot for giving good money to, as she called them, *'men in shiny suits, bearing gifts'*. It felt really good to be taking some positive action at last and whenever I make a decision I will often run with it, probably influenced by a quote I spotted many years ago that most people will relate to - *'It's Debilitating to Dither'*.

Testing the Bathwater

Men in Shiny Suits Bearing Gifts

Jane thought I had completely lost my marbles for wanting to see these 'snake oil salesmen' so I had to pretty much drag her down to Heathrow a few weeks later. She was trying hard to persuade me to carry on into London to catch a show - I had just read *Les Misérables* and she knew I was keen I to see the live show. It was a bright sunny day, the sun roof was open and the last thing she wanted to do was spend it stuck it a seminar with people trying to liberate us from our hard earned money. She very nearly convinced me but I was really determined to find a way out of my old work life, it was that or I resigned myself to a life of quiet desperation.

Like divine intervention I suddenly remembered a line I had recently read whilst dredging around the internet and tried it out on Jane. I waited for the appropriate moment and spoke in the most solemn voice I could muster - *'Jane, what if, what we do today, changes what we do for the rest of our lives?'* I knew it had hit the mark as Jane went very quiet and gazed out the window for some time, oblivious to the wind whipping at her hair. She didn't complain when I indicated and turned off at the Heathrow junction.

We parked the car and walked to the hotel entrance with no idea of what to expect. At this point I had never sat in a seminar or any type of training environment since I left school. There at the door to greet us, wearing their shiny suits, were the two company directors. Jane was impressed by the warmth of their greeting and the genuine smiles. By the end of the day we were both blown away by what I described as their 'Attitude of Abundance' (that word again). My plan for the day was to grab as much information as I could, perhaps even splash out on a book, and scurry back to Somerset to see if I could implement it. But the little voice in my head was telling me that free or almost free stuff, is usually free for a reason and if you genuinely wanted to change the direction of your life for the better (and possibly that of your descendants) then you just may have to bite the bullet, open your wallet and get some serious training and possibly buy into a quality ongoing mentorship.

Fast forward and to date I have spent circa £25k+ on my property education and personal development and would do it again in a heartbeat. I am, therefore more than a little flummoxed at some people's refusal to get some good quality property education before setting sail to spend humongous amounts of money on investment properties. I have witnessed the disastrous results of deals that have gone bad or simply never materialised through lack of information and support. Really good quality training courses are available for anywhere between £600 and £5k - all tax deductable. I firmly believe that investing in yourself is the best investment you can make not only for yourself but also for your family's future and it is something that you never stop.

I was quite surprised to find us driving home at the end of the day making plans for Jane to accept the offer of redundancy from the local authority, where she had been working as an accountant. I in turn was going to ease out of my J.O.B. Radical! We didn't expect that! We would also sign up for the forthcoming 3 day 'Masterclass' in property investing and we would give some serious consideration to the new 12 month mentorship on offer. (I had already decided I wanted to do it but didn't want to scare off Jane - one step at a time eh?). The following Monday when a member of the sales team called me to tell me the price and to take the payment I had cooled off a little and changed my mind. I told him that for now I was happy with the two £15 books I had bought at the event and when he pressed me I said 'I'll think about it'! Which we all know means 'No thanks!' Ha! No way was I going to pay £1,000s for information that I could get free off the internet - my Mama didn't raise no fool!

Mahatma Gandhi said: 'Your beliefs become your thoughts, your thoughts become your words, your words become your actions, your actions become your habits, your habits become your values and your values become your destiny'

I got on with my day but a few hours later stopped in my tracks and said out loud *'Francis you are such an idiot!'* I wanted a better life, I wanted change and I had been shown the door, but what did I do, I walked right past it. I was focusing on the price of the training and not considering the cost to me and my family of me not doing it. If I wanted change the first thing that had to change was me. I called right back and booked two places on the forthcoming Masterclass. It felt surreal and made me a little nauseous, partly as I knew that I would later have to explain my decision to Jane!! Double Eeek!

The reality of it was that Jane was now on the same wavelength as me. Later that day we talked about how it is odd that people will spend a fortune on a house, a holiday and a car but nothing on improving themselves, and 'they' are the ones who have to pay for all that other stuff! Once you rediscover the true value for yourself and your family

88

of constant improvement and education, you will never stop and never look at the world with the same eyes.

Another way to look at it is this; 'Crash' and 'Collision' more or less mean the same thing until you put the word 'Course' after them. We chose to do a Crash Course - the 3 day event was only the beginning - whereas so often I meet people who have a strange aversion to paying any money whatsoever to get even a basic understanding of the property industry. They then go out and spend sometimes hundreds of thousands of pounds which puts them on a Collision Course and ends up costing them far more in time, money and especially the big one - emotional pain.

The Property Masterclass

... who are these people?

It was October 4th 2009 and I felt like I'd just joined a kind of secret cult (it still feels like that at times). Jane and I travelled to Wokefield Park in Berkshire on our wedding anniversary no less, to spend three days with the guys in shiny suits and a group of people we had never met ... they were all going to be weirdos, weren't they? It took me till lunchtime on the first day to relax and settle in and then I moved to the front for the afternoon session. As the three days went by I felt like I was being given the keys to the secret underground world of property investing and better still it was fun! I met some brilliant people at that event and have in fact been on holiday with five of them, no less. (Not on my own you understand!)

Since that event I have willingly paid tens of thousands of pounds in various training fees and have been repaid by my investments many times over. I have a rule; if I don't double my investment Jane gets to call me a Muppet again, and I don't like it when she does that so it makes me work real hard! The properties I own, or control, allow me to spend my days as I want. I am building a wealth-base foundation for me and for my family. I still work hard but it's completely different now. When you have a good solid foundation you can build and build and build. Even if I hadn't made a penny, the friends and the people I've been fortunate to meet over the last 3 years, have enriched me and made me look at life in a completely different way. You have made it all a worthwhile journey and I thank you for the inspiration.

We left the training feeling all fired up (and a tadge overwhelmed) with a plan of action. We then made the classic mistake - we tried to do *everything*. Buy below market value properties, do assisted sales, lease options, delayed completions, we looked at Multi-Let properties for the super-charged cash-flow, and in the first three months we did ... less than nothing! Have you ever watched a stupid dog chasing its own tail? That was us! So we stopped, regrouped and decided we were going to stick to one strategy just like we were taught to do (F.O.C.U.S. = Follow One Course Until Successful). We decided we were going to buy two and three bedroom properties at below market value, then refurbish and remortgage them to get as much money as possible back out again so that we could repeat the process. We had some equity in our own property that we could access to start the ball rolling and it was time to put that training into practice and off we went spiralling right outside our comfort zone on the property rollercoaster. Whooo Hooo!

Big and Hairy

... and audacious

Some wise people I have met along the way told me to set both short term targets and long term goals but not to get too tangled up in obtaining them. It's about the journey not the destination! (Cliché alert!) But pausing for a moment here and there to smell the roses and enjoy the moment is something a lot of property investors forget to do and something I am only just beginning to get to grips with it. Most people I have met in property set goals for the following 12 months. I think this is way too short a time-frame in property terms. Most people seem to overestimate what they can achieve in a year and underestimate what they can achieve in 10 years. Set a big hairy goal, break it down into bite sized chunks, celebrate as you go to 'anchor' success in your mind and then set ever bigger and more audacious goals as you grow in confidence. If you don't set a destination how will you know where you are along the journey and when you have reached it, and how can you celebrate it? The reason I now set goals is because I like to reward myself and celebrate.

To be perfectly honest with you I didn't really set goals that first year - I really didn't know the industry, how long anything would take or even if it would work at all. I decided that I would just *'go for it'* and make as many audacious offers to estate agents as possible, then crack on with the refurbs at lightning speed and get the remortgages done as soon as possible. I was very fortunate to find a great mortgage adviser at second attempt; the first one was dreadful so I went fishing on the internet, where else?

I found myself doing and thinking about things in a way that most people don't do. I was pretty much back in full time education and loving it, I would give up my evenings, weekends and sometimes my holidays to either attend or support property and other training events. Most, well actually *all*, of my friends and family thought I had totally lost the plot. (Maybe they were right!) It may have been easier for me as I had been self -employed for many years and am quite self-motivated, but one thing is for sure; once you start, you just can't go back to being 'most people', it is totally impossible to unentrepreneuralise yourself!

As the year went by I grew in confidence and by December I had bought eight properties. Eight properties!! I had not slowed down to take a breath and when I did I was in shock. Wow, where did all those properties come from? But did it all go smoothly, well yes and no - there is always space for a little more Mayhem! So here is a quick snap-shot of the following 18 months before I discovered the awesome power of Multi-Lets and then the Rent to Rent system that Emily and I later honed to perfection. Most of the properties we bought were smooth sailing; the departing owners were great, the refurbs were fast and efficient and good tenants moved in. Due to past events this felt a little weird and I was forever waiting for 'something' to happen but it never did, at least not with five of them, as for the other three …

Welcome to the UK

... and the winter of discontent

> *I love this little negotiation joke:* 'I have a really smart dog and taught him how to play cards. He's rubbish at it - every time he has a good hand his tail starts wagging!'

Our first Below Market Value (BMV) deal was a two bedroom terraced property that was advertised with a local agent who I had been building a relationship with (this is very important as people like to do business first and foremost with people they like). The elderly couple who owned the property were mortgage free and had moved on as soon as they received an offer on the property. They didn't realise that many offers fell through as this and the next two did. This is all gold-dust information that most agents will not tell you - unless you have a good relationship with them! The property was advertised at £100k for a fast sale and this was a good price. We offered £75k and said we could complete to suit their timescale, were 100% committed and wouldn't drop out like previous offers - these words are magical to agents and vendors. This offer was refused as was our next offer of £77.5k.

When offering on properties it is generally accepted that you follow the Verisimilitude principle. The definition in the dictionary is 'the appearance of being real or true'. If

I offered £75k, then £76k, then £77k it's pretty obvious that those numbers were just pulled out a hat and there was probably more where that came from. Whereas if I offered £75k, £77.5k and make my final offer £78,247 (I told the agent this was after I had spoken to my bank manager and broker to see what was the absolute maximum I could raise!) that makes it all sound very real and believable.

As it was the agent told me that £80k would seal the deal and more offers were coming in. Although I trusted the agent I knew he was obliged to act in the owners' best interest so took this with a pinch of salt but this was still a very good price so we agreed. It later revalued at £110k.

The refurb was completed in a week and we signed in a lovely African couple who were new to England. They stayed with us for 9 months and I have to be honest and say we didn't do one interim inspection back then. (We have systemised all this now) and so didn't hear from them from the start to the end of the tenancy, after a very long and cold winter.

When we met at the property to sign them out, I instantly remarked how cold the place was and asked if the heating was working OK? Their mood completely changed, they started looking very awkward and told me they were hardly ever home. Huh? I checked the boiler and saw that the pressure was at zero. I asked them how long it had been like that. The guy was kicking his heels and said it had never really worked and that was part of the reason they were moving on. What! I checked the pipe-work under the sink and found a small leak which had caused the water pressure to drop and the boiler to switch off. The tenants were looking very sheepish - I guess they thought it was their fault and would lose their deposit. When I reassured them it was not their fault and that I would have fixed this little problem months ago if they had called me and that they would get their deposit back in a few days, they relaxed and the big smiles returned. I admired their eventual honesty but thought that in this case, insanity would have been a better defence. I could easily imagine them getting stuck in a revolving door for hours.

The whole winter with no heating or hot water! What must they have thought of the UK and those mean old landlords? They had probably been listening to their Grandfathers tales of Peter Rachman! (If you don't know who he is, Google him).

Red Red Wine

The Wrath of Grapes

Alison had just separated from her husband and moved into our newly refurbed property number three with her two young teenage daughters. On a good day she was very smart and very pleasant, but on a crummy day she looked and acted like a bad tempered Chihuahua that had been tumbled dried!

The first time I met her it was the middle of winter and even though she was wearing a thin tee shirt she looked very hot - temperature wise I mean! I noticed this each time we met.

I always leave a few small maintenance jobs to do after the tenant has moved in - so that I can stop by to make sure all is as it should be. The first thing I noticed was the huge pile of empty wine bottles placed beside the overflowing recycle box. I mean 'huge'! I asked 'Had a party'? She just smiled. When I saw the same mountain of bottles appearing every week I stopped asking and posted some information from Alcoholics Anonymous through her door - anonymously of course. She must have been spending an absolute fortune on wine and I could see her health and mood were suffering. Her poor girls were always on the receiving end of a totally unnecessary cutting remark from a hung-over Alison, which made her just look foolish to me. Many things can be preserved in alcohol; dignity is not one of them!

The property had been empty and was owned by Persimmons, one of the big house building companies when I bought it. The previous owner had lived there for some time and had wanted to buy a brand new home (I could never see the sense in that, it's like buying a brand new car - you always have to pay a premium). Often the builders were desperate to sell their stock and so would do a part exchange and they sometimes made miscalculations, as 'second hand stock' was not their area of expertise. This property had no central heating and only partial double glazing. Persimmons (and I) didn't see this as a major problem but all the people who had viewed it to this point, and there had been many, did see it as a problem. It was overpriced at £120k and I made a cheeky offer of £80k which, as expected was refused. I knew the builder was desperate to sell and that the agent was fed up with doing viewings so I sat back and waited.

Buying property can sometimes be like playing poker - you have to hold your nerve. Some of our best deals have come from 'pipelining', where you track a property with the agent. Statistics vary but some say up to 50% of deals fall out of bed and return to the market due to mortgage offers being turned down, buyer getting cold feet or them having another offer accepted elsewhere. So a month later when the agent called me back to ask if I was still interested and would I like to resubmit my offer, I lowered it to £77k due to market conditions etc., (i.e. I had all the power) and this time the offer was instantly accepted.

Whenever I called at the house it was always cold as Alison said she couldn't afford to turn on the heating, (she liked expensive wine!). So her two girls often sat there freezing cold in their hats, coats and fingerless gloves doing their homework while mum sat there sweating and guzzling a bottle of Merlot or Shiraz. Alison's brow was never without beads of running moisture and she always had the appearance of someone trying to sweat out a fever.

98

There were always big pans boiling away on the stove whenever I called - I mentioned that the extraction fan should be switched on, but to save money Alison opened a window - much to the girl's chagrin, who more than likely closed it seconds after I left with their teeth chattering away, the poor wee things.

All none of my business you might say - true - until all this extra moisture, lack of ventilation and lack of heating manifested itself as damp patches appearing all over the ground floor. I was informed of this at month five when she gave her notice to leave - she said 'couldn't live in these conditions!' When she left a month later, the damp problem and the mountain of wine bottles left with her. It is true that many a good whine comes from sour grapes!

Being a builder I totally understood the importance of access to constant Cash flow for any business and so for that and other reasons we decided to flip (sell) this property. We had owned it for only seven months and banked a clear £23k net profit. I liked this property investing stuff!

International Relations

... and the house of ill repute

Deal number seven was the best deal (I read somewhere that you don't get what you deserve, you get what you negotiate!) and without doubt the most hilarious. It was advertised at £110k and we eventually agreed a price of £77k. The property owner, a lady who went by the name of Chantelle (at times she was also known as Dixie, Claudia, Roxy, Candy and Angel) had already moved on, so we were dealing only with the agent who could only be described as an amateur and a serial lying imbecile. If not for the fact it was such a good deal I would have told him what he could do with his property many times, and had to constantly remind myself that this was not a romantic date, it was a business transaction! The refurb cost £15k and the property eventually revalued at £125k, which meant we got all the money back out with enough over for a quick excursion to Barcelona. Cool.

The overgrown garden at the back of the property had been untouched for so many years that it was now like a mini Amazon that David Attenborough would have been happy to explore. Whilst hacking our way through we discovered two canoes complete with paddles (ebay'ed them), 10 big steel drums (scrap yard), two also new racing bikes (second hand shop), and a load of expensive fishing equipment (Dave the labourer had that). But possibly the most interesting find was a box of letters and photos we found in the house behind a beam in the attic room that had not been used for years. There were no stairs and it could only be accessed with a ladder so Chantelle either forgot it was there or planted it for us to find. We would have tried to return them to Chantelle via the agent but apparently she got extremely aggressive when the purchase was delayed for a week so we didn't bother - she may have taken it the wrong way! It was obvious that the agent was petrified of her and would probably have binned it anyway.

There were constantly five or six guys on site as I wanted to get the large refurb done as swiftly as possible, and it was inevitable that light entertainment would be added at break times by someone delving into Chantelle's box. Dave felt it was his moral duty and claimed he was only looking for a forwarding address. Conclusion number one - she was definitely on the game! It was all carefully chronicled in her letters with accompanying photos. Where are my surgical gloves? Yuk!

February - She meets a young Spanish guy on Facebook named Juan and invites him to England. (No mention to Juan of what she did for a living at this point). April - he duly arrives. Happy days! Juan had a beaming smile, his hair was short he seemed oblivious to the large age gap between him and Chantelle. May arrived and everything was great - especially now Chantelle is pregnant with Juan's baby. More photos- Juan is holding the baby - his hair is longer, the smile is still there but Juan looks tired and jaded. More letters and Dave can now do a pretty good impersonation of Juan (in the style of Manuel from Faulty Towers). Things are obviously a tadge strained between Chantelle and Juan as he discovers and documents what she gets up to while he is out working at the local banana factory.

His hair had by now almost reached his shoulders and the forced smile looks more like a pained grimace. The final photo of the loving couple, now plus bambino, shows

Juan's teeth exposed in what is obviously a snarl! He left for Spain soon after and she was left holding the baby. A further batch of unsent letters held together with an elastic band, exposed her as an extremely enraged, aggressive and a vengeful creature as she promised to *'hunt Juan down all over the planet - Juan could run but he couldn't hide'!* Eek, Run Juan Run!!

From the amount of debt letters arriving at the property after we had the keys, it was clear that Juan was meant to be her meal ticket now that her *'business has slackened off'* a little. The property was on the verge of being repossessed when I bought it. There had been many viewings but no other offers. This was more than likely due to Chantelle's attempt at home improvements - those daytime TV programmes have a lot to answer for! To the untrained eye the property looked a wreck - she had decided to go for the open plan stairs look, so she ripped out all the spindles, a door, a frame, a supporting beam and cut the newel post in half! Consequently going up the stairs was like having a go on the House of Fun at the local funfair! Everything was moving and parts of it were held together with Duct tape. (Duct tape has always figured big in my life too!) But the reality was that it only took me an afternoon to sort out. I love these types of properties as they look much worse that they really are - you have to be able to see through the mess, have your team ready, *get all your ducks in a row* and attack the job full on from the moment you have the keys!

We had a lot of interest for this property and selected a young couple with a baby. We asked one of the mothers to act as a guarantor and all went smoothly with their tenancy ... except for the time a really rough looking guy hammered on the door late one evening. He was drunk, said he had just got out of prison and wanted to speak to his mum who lives there. He was calling my tenant Juan and said he didn't look very Spanish. He wouldn't believe that his mum had moved on without informing him and took a lot of convincing that she wasn't just hiding in the property. He kept shouting over my tenant's shoulder to *'stop mucking about mum and come to the door'*. He said his mum's real name was Susan and that she owed him a lot of money! He eventually left when the tenant threatened to call the police! The worried tenant put up a surveillance camera.

That Feeling of Abundance

... or the lack thereof!

Abundance is a wonderful word; its synonyms are fortune, luxury, opulence, plenty, prosperity, riches and wealth. But it doesn't have to be all about money; it can be an abundance of information, education, love or friendships. I love abundance!

> *I was on a Ryan Air flight recently and it soon became apparent that abundance was going to be scarce on that flight! I'll swear they periodically move the seats marginally closer together to pack more people onto the planes. They seem to have perfected the art of making an unpleasant experience worse and I heard that they now are even thinking of charging schizophrenics for two seats! It's criminal.*

Back to the plot: so we had secured some single let properties that were all let with good tenants. We had flipped a property and made a good amount of Cash flow, and Emily was running the student Multi-Let with no problems. I felt great and knew my life had taken a different trajectory. We were always jetting off, OK driving off, to various networking and mentoring events all over the UK and meeting our new friends. I saw it all as a big

104

adventure and was excited as to what the future would bring. I guess James and Emily must have noticed a change in me with my new found energy and enthusiasm - I was meeting some amazing and totally inspiring people almost every week. Something I noticed about these new humans almost immediately was how positive and open they were. There was a real sense of community and I found it so refreshing that everyone was always willing to listen and jump in with offers of assistance. There was a real attitude of abundance and I found myself being drawn to the company of these people more and more.

Around this time I also noticed a certain degree of negativity in some of the people I had known for years. We are without doubt a by-product of the people we spend most of our time with, so be careful who you choose for friends!

During the final year of Emily's Architecture degree she had been reading a few of my new books, including *Rich Dad Poor Dad* by Robert Kiyosaki. Like most people who read this book Emily had an epiphany and decided that working the next 20 years in an architect's practice was not for her. The entrepreneurial light had been switched on! She called Jane and booked a meeting (this sounded serious!). She said she wanted to join Jane and me in the family business, and although I dearly wanted to say yes, I had to say no as we were not really earning enough to support ourselves let alone Emily. Property investing is a long term strategy and any exit from a salaried job should be carefully planned. I have attended many events where there is a big cheer when someone announces they have 'sacked their boss' - which could also mean that they are now pretty much unmortgageable and if they don't build cash flow fast could soon be in dire financial straits! In hindsight I can see that I gave up my building work six months too soon and we did struggle with money for a little while. (Until Emily and I eventually discovered a brilliant way to boost our cash flow really fast!)

So I declined Emily's request to work with us, instead I gave her some more property and inspirational books to read from my growing library, and she reluctantly found a 9 to 5 office job. She also started looking for a more professional house-share to move into, as four years of student life was more than enough for her. After a frustrating three months of searching she realised that there were in fact very few properties to choose from and the standard of the ones she did view was appalling - she always brought some hand-wash with her and often found herself wiping her feet on the way out of most of the houses! Emily and I talked about this and realised there was a huge gap in the market for good quality house-shares for professionals but unfortunately we had no money to buy, no confidence to do a joint venture and didn't understand the power of bridging or commercial finance. So we pushed it to the back of our minds.

A few months later Emily and Jane attended a training day that they had won at a local networking event, and spent the day with another great property training professional Simon Zutshi. It was a taster day and Simon had briefly mentioned something about a process called 'Let to Let' which Emily found intriguing. She called me and we agreed to meet up the next day to see if we could find out what it was all about. In actual fact I jumped right on to my computer and didn't move from the spot for the next four hours. I discovered that Let to Let had been around for a very long time and was also known as Guaranteed Rent or more prominently, Rent to Rent.

What is Rent to Rent?

... Baking a cake with random ingredients

Mention Rent to Rent to some letting agents and they will think 'sub-let' and therein lies the first problem - 'sublet' has become an erroneous term - probably made so by unfortunate agents who, in the past, had to clear up the detritus left over from illegal and badly set up tenancies. Getting agents and sometimes owners, to accept that we are offering a solution that will greatly benefit ALL parties can, at times, be an uphill struggle. But when they finally 'get it', they generally put us at the top of their Christmas card list.

We offer our services as a specialist Multi Let agent and generally work with distressed owners and sometimes overstretched agents. Most properties that we take over have a problem of sorts that we have to fix - whether it be the condition of the property or the management. Owners may be absent, disinterested or simply overwhelmed by their responsibilities and many local agents are just not geared up to operate Multi-Let properties.

A very low input is required by the investor, and the profit produced can be 5 times that of a single let. A downside to this may be that the investor will never benefit from equity growth and that the property owner may take the property back after the investor has carried out a refurb. But there are ways to mitigate this risk.

Digging out information about Rent to Rent was not an easy task, it was almost like this insider knowledge was being protected and hidden away from the general public. At a very basic level and as the name implies you rent a property from someone and then you rent out the rooms individually, guaranteeing the owner his rent whether the rooms are filled or not. So the risk lies entirely with you and you must also take care of all the tenants and any problems that may arise along the way. On the surface this seemed pretty easy, but if that were the case why was it not mainstream and why were more people not doing it? I was to find out exactly why that was over the next twelve months.

Emily and I started researching the area. Another student year was approaching and although the usual large Victorian properties were coming onto the market they were not being snapped up as quickly as normal. We knew this was partly due to the Government and the Uni's finally realising that there was money to be made by building new dedicated student blocks on campus up and down the country. The knock-on effect of this was that the old landlords that historically did not have to try too hard to fill their properties now had them sitting empty. We spotted rather a lot of them and noticed that the asking price was dropping each month, signs of desperation from either the landlord or the agents.

Next we looked at the demand for rooms and what was happening with the economy. Mortgages were getting increasingly difficult to secure as lending criteria tightened, there was more job insecurity, more immigration and it seemed young professionals had no desire to return home to Mummy and Daddy's house - I experienced this firsthand! What all this meant was that it was a golden age for landlords in general and especially so for those with rooms to rent - it is like all your stars being in alignment or the perfect storm.

108

But did the numbers all add up? The last property I bought had cost me an £18k deposit and £3k for legal fees plus a small refurbishment, so £21k in all. This property generates £250 net cash each month or £3k per year. In one year, after numerous attempts to repair it, I replaced the boiler, put up some new fencing and had to retile the kitchen. This cost around £2k which leaves me a profit of £1k or £83 per month, how many of these would you need to become financially independent? Quite a few, and one more major repair or a hike in interest rates would wipe out all my profit. A property like this may be good for long term capital growth but not much good for cash flow right now!

Emily and I carried on researching and came to the conclusion that we could set up a Rent to Rent property in Bristol where Emily lives for around £3.5k, and it would generate a net profit in the region of £650 per month. So that same £21k we used to buy the single let property could secure six Rent to Rent properties for us and generate a cash flow of around £3,900 net per calendar month. So that's £89 or £3.9k. Wow! Our eyebrows hit the ceiling and our jaws hit the floor! We were gobsmacked at the numbers and set to work immediately formulating a plan of action.

We made a list of properties we were interested in; made a list of ten agents, had a think and made a note of what we were going to say and planned out the day. There are a few reasons why Monday is not a good day to approach an agent, so Tuesday morning it was. We were bubbling with confidence - this was going to be life changing and we were excited!

Failure is Not an Option

... Welcome on board the steam train

So we weren't really sure what we doing or what we were getting ourselves into, but I have always had a rule in life; if you must do a foolish thing, do it with enthusiasm!

This was going to be so brilliant and we felt that total exhilaration that you get just after a great idea hits you and just before you figure out what is wrong with it!

Tuesday arrived and it felt like the first day of school - we both felt excited and apprehensive in equal measures and were raring to go. We parked the car, confidently marched up to the first agent on our list to announce our intentions and ... walked right past, as we decided to go for a coffee (i.e. we bottled it!). I gave Emily a pep-talk over a green tea and flapjack and we tried again, this time I strode boldly to the shop, I was brimming with renewed confidence as I grabbed the door handle, swung the door open and pushed Emily in! What a coward!

We are often asked if it is a good idea to make initial contact with agents via phone or in person. From what we experienced over the next 3 hours we decided that phone is the better option. An agent stood and greeted us and we set about our first attempt to explain ourselves. We had no script and there were no Rent to Rent trainings for us to attend to hone our skills. The agent's eyes and general demeanour quickly took on the appearance of an extra in a zombie movie. The noise of the office quietened to a whispered hush. I was speaking with confidence but knew it was a lost cause as the agent kept cutting me off and saying in a condescending voice *'yes but that is sub-letting'* (I half expected him to add *'my dear boy'*). To many old school letting agents, the mere mention of the word 'sublet' will cause them to involuntary suck air through their teeth and shake their head from side to side as they recoil backwards.

The new world order: Most agents have been trained and conditioned to do one thing and that is to work their butts off for a 10% share of the rental income, and while it may be a great job and a busy life it's not going to make the average agent wealthy. Rent to Rent is a completely different model that enables you to take control of a property, if needed furnish it and even carry out a light refurb, for up to a 50% share of the rental income. Why would anyone not choose the latter? One infuriated independent agent said to me as he walked me towards the door *'I have been doing this job for twenty years and have never ... blah blah'* (There was a lot of emphasis on 'twenty'). As he spoke I noticed his shabby suit and the ten year old Skoda parked outside, the shop also needed an update. I thought to myself he has actually been doing the job for one year and repeating it for nineteen, blind to any new opportunity.

The morning didn't go well for Emily and I and by one o'clock we were feeling like a couple of deflated airbeds and so decided to return home. We couldn't understand why the agents weren't going for it as it would actually make their lives easier in the long run. Jane was surprised to see us. I refused her offer of a cup of tea and instead went to sit in a darkened room for fifteen minutes. Doh!

We actually never felt defeated as we knew Rent to Rent is a brilliant strategy, we just had to figure out a script, work out a system and find some agents that were on the same wavelength as us. This *had* to work as we didn't have any plan B! (I suspect that the only reason most people have a plan B is because deep down in their soul they suspect plan A will fail!)

This took us two solid months of calling agents, solicitors, landlords, local council officers, talking to professional associations, research, research, research. When we had worked out a script we tried it on agents out of our area and we decided to *'Go for no'*. You know when someone is really desperate for something you can sometimes detect it in their voice? Well we decided for a bit of fun to turn the whole thing on its head and see who could collect the most 'No's' before they got a 'Yes'. As it was, the second agent I called readily agreed to meet with me. I double checked that he had fully understood me, he had, but there was a slight problem as he was in the Midlands! I said I'd check with my business partner and get back to him.

Now we started calling local agents to book viewings. All but one was happy with what we were saying and so over the course of the next month we viewed around fifty properties. We could have easily lost control at this point and had to quickly work out a system to identify which properties worked, what they needed and all related costs to be able to work out if it was a deal or not. We now have a Rent to Rent deal analyser to do this - punch in the numbers and your criteria and you get a simple yes or a no.

We also had to quickly find a contract that the agents and owners accepted and that was going to work for us too. This was no simple task as we had no trusted mentor to offer advice and the three solicitors we asked all had a different point of view. Our property solicitor is great at scrutinising contracts - she totally understands that *education* is when you read the fine print and *experience* is what you get when you don't!

Fast forward: the debate of which contract to use with Rent to Rent deals has been raging back and forth on many forums since we did our first training event. It would seem that each contract has its pro's and con's and it supporters and detractors. I actually think that the perfect contract has not yet been created and with this in mind, I am currently in talks with my solicitor.

Five months later we had secured 9 Rent to Rent properties that were bringing in a cool £5,000 net profit each and every month. So where does the steam train analogy come in? Well, we pretty much shut off from everything in the world for the two months of research, the five months securing the properties and a further month to streamline and get everything up to speed so that it ran like a well-oiled machine. Even though we started with no help and no previous experience, we were like an unstoppable steam train - nothing was going to get in our way and nothing was going to stop us from reaching our target of £5,000! There were many obstacles and many critics along the way - in fact there still are - but we just stayed focused, had total belief and kept on going, getting a little closer every day. If you have not already, you must read/listen to the Slight Edge by Jeff Olson.

We started tweaking the nine properties and the rents and soon increased that cash flow to over £6k. This is something we are always looking at - reducing costs and increasing profits. You probably know the Apollo analogy about all the rockets only being on target for 3% of the time, the other 97% of the time they were making corrections to their course. Business and even life is like this - there are no straight lines and so for maximum efficiency you must be forever making small corrections.

Blam! 50 Tenants

Adventures in Wonderland

We had done it; we had built the cash flow we wanted well within the timeframe we set ourselves. What kind-of surprised us and crept up on us was that we picked up 50 tenants along the way! The last six months had really tested us both and we each discovered some personal strengths and weaknesses. Emily soon discovered she preferred dealing with the business side of things to dealing with tenants. This was OK because even with my previous tenant experiences, I was very much a people person. But with so many people to look after we had to systemise everything and we had to do it fast. We checked out what everyone else was doing with an intention to 'borrow' as much as we could (take from one and it's theft, take from many and it's research!) but found everything to be stuffy and formal and really not our style. So we got busy creating our own business manual and thinking of every way possible to make our lives easier. It was working very well.

One particular Thursday Emily and I found we had 14 rooms to fill (don't ask!) and whilst everything at the shop-front appeared smooth and calm, behind the scenes it was complete bedlam, but somehow we managed to fill 8 rooms between sunrise and sunset. Result! We now built up a variety of strategies that we can employ to get rooms filled fast and in fact have not had a room sat empty for more than a day, except for maintenance, for some time.

I could say that everything went really well, everything was fine and dandy and we never had a problem. But life is rarely like that and if you are like me you soon tire of the BS (belief system) that some people continually gush about, everything always being perfect. The reality was that we made some mistakes with the properties we took over and mistakes with some of the tenants we allowed to move into them. The difference was that this time we were instantly onto any problem and it was normally taken care of within 24 hours. This is the best, in fact, the only way to deal with complaints from tenants.

We have 4, 5 and 6 bed properties that house our tenants and we try to match them up as far as possible with regards to age and tenant type. For instance we would try not to house a construction worker with a doctor, and I realise that this sweeping generalisation may insult any construction workers reading this as well it may insult any doctors, but we had to work to some kind of a system. We also decided not to take on people on a low wage such as a part time waitress, as from experience I knew they would struggle to pay their way and it would lead to future heartaches when you had to ask them to depart. We turned away anyone reeking of alcohol or excessive body odour and anyone unable to prove they had a job. Our last criterion was that they had to be nice people. Define nice! Maybe 'good' would be a better word, but you only really find out what a person is like by living with them for a while, so it's always a bit like playing Russian roulette.

So what went wrong? Well it was never the mayhem of the earlier years but we did rent to a public schoolboy type who managed to alienate the other housemates within 24 hours of moving in along with the entire contents of a 2 bed house (split with posh girlfriend). He couldn't cram it all into his bedroom so it was stuffed into every nook and cranny throughout the house until the day he departed. When he left his room, it was a complete mess and from then on we decided to implement a £30 fixed cleaning charge for all vacating tenants, we pay the cleaner £15 for the clean so this is yet another little stream of income. To make things worse, although he was over 6ft tall, the rotter insisted on wearing a teddy bear onesie at all times, which was wrong on so many levels!

Jax was a normal looking French chap when he moved in and spent the next six months injecting steroids, too many steroids, which made his muscles and his eyes bulge, and it also made him very angry most of the time. Towards the end of his tenancy he had grown freakishly big so that his clothes were now all too small for him. But with the cost of all the gym candy he had been buying, he was struggling with money so had to make do with what he had. He looked like Norman Wisdom but no one would dare laugh at him (at least to his face) for fear of making him angry again. Whenever the housemates went out, poor Jax was left playing home alone and after six months of tense drama in the house, to everyone's relief, he moved on. One of the other housemates told me that he had apparently been accused of some cowardly act at home and so was determined to return ripped and shredded and all beefed out so that he could take sweet revenge! I never doubt the courage of the French, for they are the ones that discovered snails are edible!

> *We have heard a multitude of excuses for not paying the rent but soon adopted a 'No Pay No Stay' policy. We always listen intently to the tenant and then say 'sorry, but whatever is happening in your life has nothing to do with you paying your rent!'*

One tenant carefully positioned a small surveillance camera 'pen' in the bathroom to film whoever was using the shower and relay it back to their computer - the culprit was caught and asked to leave. We have had several cases of Marijuana being smoked in the house - we have a zero tolerance on this and have ejected two people pretty much on the spot. There have been a few petty cases of malicious damage and the common problem of people being too messy and or too lazy. I have seen some Multi-Let landlords get very emotional when tenants fail to respect their property and sometimes understandably so. But I decided a long time ago that I was never going to let a tenant put me in a bad mood or ruin my day, and anyway I think you should never ascribe to malice that which can be adequately explained by incompetence or stupidity. Whenever we have to talk to tenants about their bad attitude we always imagine we are talking to small children to make sure we get the message across.

> *I find it interesting how some people need to have so much 'stuff' around them and take a whole day to move in, while other people have almost no possessions. What does that tell us about personality types? One guy, a male nurse, arrived with just a backpack of possessions including one book, stayed eight months and gave me a great gift on his departure day; he said 'the best way to cheer yourself up is to cheer somebody else up'. Priceless advice.*

So it was all trucking along nicely, most of the professional tenants stayed for around nine months and there was not much hassle. I adopted a rule of 'if it moves, systemise it', and started looking for some new properties to expand our little empire. Then out of the blue I received some really shocking news.

118

MURDER

The Murder

Emily and I had set up our first 9 Multi-Let properties in Bristol over the course of five months that generated a consistent £5k net per month. It was an utterly crazy time that we both loved - we realised we had strengths we were unaware of and just how much we could achieve if we really focused and set our minds to it.

The great thing about the Rent to Rent system we are using is that if a property turns out to be a lemon you can simply hand it back at the end of the agreed term. The first property we took over turned out to be more than just a lemon - it was a complete and utter Kipper! But we were so desperate to secure our first property that we were blind to the facts; it was out of our area, difficult to get to in rush hour, had too small a kitchen, had a hard-to-let box room and the owner was a complete and utter buffoon. The signs were all there - we chose to ignore them!

By the time we had got to the end of the year we had fallen out with the owner. Amongst his misdemeanours, and there were many, he kept entering the property, and even the bedrooms, unannounced! Riff raff like him give the industry a bad name and we were only too pleased to tell him we would not be renewing the contract - he retorted by saying we would not be getting our deposit back. I guess he did that to everyone. When I pointed out he had not served us the correct deposit information when he protected the deposit and could therefore end up paying us substantially more, he coughed up the very next day. Good riddance.

There were four tenants living at this property. Two found alternative accommodation and the other two asked us to re-room them. One was a messy lady who had failed to set up a standing order despite our constant requests to do so. We told her we had no room for her. We have systems in place now that ensure standing orders are set up from day one and our rents are consistently 100% paid. But the guy, Joel, was brilliant, all paperwork in place from day one, room immaculate, house tidier since he arrived; he was always upbeat, loved reggae music and was an all-around top man who shared a pot of goat soup with me on more than one occasion. Anytime I was at the house doing viewings or taking care of any maintenance issues I would always knock his door to say hi. We got on really well and so I not only made sure we had a new room for him, I even arranged a van to move him at our expense. When you have a good tenant you must hold on to them!

Joel was Jamaican and joined the British army to escape the poverty he was experiencing at home; I think he may have had a son back in Jamaica. He had a good job with the ministry of defence and a tall, good looking girlfriend with long blond hair. He was very happy to be moving to the new property as it was a large mid terraced Victorian property with much more communal space than his first place, and, we assured him, much better housemates. Around the time Joel moved to his new house, the girlfriend decided to skedaddle and moved back home with her dad and stepmom. When I visited Joel a few days after he moved in to the new house he was very quiet and obviously upset, but made no indication to me as to why that was.

That weekend the girlfriends parents arranged to meet Joel at his house to collect the last of her possessions. No one really knows what happened but it seems raised voices were overheard and an argument ensued which soon spiralled out of control. There was one other tenant at home, playing music in her room at the back of the house.

The parents rushed out of the house and got into their car. Joel went into the kitchen and grabbed a long kitchen knife; he then ran out to the car and swung open the passenger door where the stepmom was sat. She was stabbed multiple times before the dad could drive off. She died en-route to hospital.

This was a bright Saturday afternoon on a street that is busy with both cars and pedestrians.

Police quickly arrived at the house. Joel was long gone. The lady from upstairs answered the door oblivious as to what had just happened and was totally shocked. Another tenant arrived home. Total disbelief. Police had to search the property and so forced the three remaining locked doors. The forensic squad arrived and went through the house with a fine tooth comb. They also found a replica handgun (!) and removed all the contents of Joel's room. The property was classed as a crime scene and closed down and all tenants are asked to leave for 5 days. Three of the tenants decide to leave for good and I didn't blame them - some people just can't cope with this sort of thing - one guy was an utter trembling wreck. When we eventually got the property back we had to get the doors repaired, for which the police paid, and tried to get the rooms re-let. For a week we told any prospective tenant what had just happened, which never failed to scare them away. We called a meeting with the remaining two tenants and decided that we wouldn't mention what had happened to any more prospective housemates and that if it ever came up they would break the news to their new housemates gently. There were a few moans but not too many.

Unfortunately (or perhaps fortunately) I was out of the country when this happened and received the news over the phone from the 'trembling wreck' on my way in a taxi to a family party in Galway, Ireland. This tenant's voice could be described as falsetto at the best of times but now he was entering into the vocal range of an over excited baboon! The already jittery taxi driver, who could hear every word my tenant was saying, was sweating bullets and looking more and more anxious as I loudly exclaimed *'A murder! In the street! The police! A kitchen knife!'* The driver kept his gaze on the road and put the pedal to the floor! He was so overjoyed at reaching the destination whilst still breathing that he sped away before we could pay him.

So what happened to Joel? Well, he was found in the next neighbourhood on the Sunday evening cowering behind a bush. He was tired and cold and kept repeating 'What have I done' over and over. It would seem like he totally lost it and was now full of regret. His case went to court and he was given a life sentence with a minimum of 25 years to serve. You could say he went from a 5 bed Multi-Let to a 500 bed Multi-Let, all bills included and lights out at 11p.m.

I have actually spent one night of my life in a prison cell and even though it was of my own choosing, I didn't particularly enjoy it.

So am I a good judge of character? The truth is you never can tell. I once read that 'Property is not really about property at all, it's about people'. At the time I thought that was nonsense, but I soon realised that it was absolutely true. People are the lifeblood of this industry and you will more than likely have to deal with every type at one time or another.

I'm often asked if this was upsetting and how I coped. It was obviously a horrible situation to have to deal with in every sense, the poor lady didn't deserve to die and there was no excuse. Yes we were upset with having to deal with the inevitable fallout, but I have never been one to bring my problems home with me. In the early days Jane could never understand why nothing seemed to rattle me. I'll tell you

124

why. I have a virtual shoebox, it didn't use to have a lid but I later realised the lid was very important! Some people are plagued by their troubles 24/7. It's the last thing on their mind and keeping them awake at night and the first thing on their mind when they open their eyes in the morning. When I shut my eyes at night I imagine all that bad stuff being put into a shoebox - it always fits - and then I put the lid on it and put it away. (I used to put it under the bed but that was too close!) Then I can forget all about it, it's still there for whenever I need to access it, but I'm not carrying it around with me taking up valuable headspace all the time. It works, try it. Now I can do it anytime day or night. When Jane upsets me, as she does from time to time I have been known to say *'Right! That's going in the shoebox!'* in my best Basil Fawlty voice.

MULTI-LETS

Shutting Everything Down

... and the Trinity of despair

As a kid did you ever hold a magnifying glass over some dry grass on a bright sunny day? This is a favourite pastime of kids everywhere, but I was always an impatient little urchin. Many a time when nothing was happening, I would be just about to give up when suddenly there would be a plume of smoke followed by a burst of flames and I would be excitedly jumping up and down fanning the mini inferno and fervently hoping I hadn't just started a summer forest fire. All I had to do was *STAY FOCUSED*, and now suddenly you know where this is going!

Ninety days. Could you go without any newspapers, TV or even turning on the radio for ninety days? Up until 2010 I lived on a staple diet of these three messengers of wretched despondency and never considered the alternative until one day I heard a successful businessman state they were not only unnecessary but a grinding drain and a scandalous distraction! He said he rarely even carried a phone. How could anyone survive in this age without constant access to a phone? I pondered on his words for some time.

I was never one of those people who religiously bought a newspaper but usually got to read one at least every other day. It always amazed me that just enough news happened each and every day to fill a newspaper - it's not like they would just make up a lot of stuff is it? 'TV addict' is a term we are all familiar with and it is generally accepted that too much TV is not good for anyone. For some people TV is a comfort that they like to hear quietly in the background, like an old friend. I would turn it on to watch a programme or film and then when it was over I would channel surf. Sound familiar? The final member of my *Trinity of Despair* is radio, of which I spent 20 of my adult years listening to every day whether I liked it or not - this was life on a building site. The choice was either Radio 1 or Radio 2 depending on who had the gumption to set up their radio first. I was never a fan of Radio 1 (That's not real music!) and so had to accept Terry Wogan on Radio 2 and resist the constant urge to hurl the radio off the scaffolding as he repeated the same 10 jokes over and over again throughout those years.

As a builder all this was fine as I knew my job well and could do most of it on auto pilot. But when I decided to leave that life behind me and focus my time, my skills and my attention on learning how to become a property investor, all that had to change, partly because I desperately needed to free up some more time. So overnight I stopped listening to the radio and stopped reading newspapers and magazines. I also reduced my TV time to one occasional American escapism series and the odd epic movie. Guess what happened? Absolutely nothing!

The world didn't stop turning, no-one came hammering on my door insisting I reinstate my subscriptions and Mr Wogan carried on oblivious to me tuning out. In fact I realised that 99.9% of what happened in the world had no bearing on my life whatsoever and me listening or reading all this doom and gloom (as most news is) would only fill my consciousness with a soul sucking and despairing view of the world. What it also meant for me was that I had many more hours in every day to spend finding deals, working with agents and most importantly working on myself. I also stopped reading fiction and have now grown a nice little library of property and personal development books, fifty per cent of which are audios that I play in the gym or on journeys. No one ever mentions the down side of this - you hear something great that you want to write down but you can't as you are driving or running and try desperately as you might later on to remember it, the words never return, at least not often! The Trinity of despair now has no interest for me whatsoever and when I think of all the time I wasted doing what I was conditioned to do, I shudder.

When Emily and I were setting up our initial Rent to Rent properties we were 100% focused. That's a term you often hear - 100% this, 100% that - but it's not often that anyone is seriously and totally committed. A great way to motivate yourself is to create a problem that you will then have to fix. We paid deposits on properties at an alarming rate and then either had to get them up to scratch and the rooms filled or we would, as they say, 'go belly up'!

The Information Age: like most other people I always thought that the advent of the Age of Information was a wonderful thing until I realised just how distracting it is. We are constantly bombarded by messages that take our mind away from the task in hand and then we spend ten minutes trying to refocus. Multiply this by twenty distractions and we end up losing many precious hours every day! When I have constant interruptions all day my head feels like a ball of wool that the cats been playing with - completely unravelled. I found the best way to focus on a task is to take yourself and your laptop away somewhere quiet and leave your phone behind. Put up a *'Do not disturb'* sign, do not access your emails or social media and don't be such an inquisitive little monkey. Gulp!

131

In fact why not take it one step further - could you survive without your phone for 10 days? Does the thought make your legs go all wobbly? I needed some distraction - free time (to write this book!) and thought I would try this when I recently went to stay with some friends in Florida. It did feel a little strange leaving it behind but after 2 days of fretting and feeling irritated I actually started enjoying the *freedom*. My son James checked my emails at home every few days and said he would contact me if there was anything urgent - there wasn't. The need to be instantly contactable 24/7 is an unnecessary and sometimes counterproductive product of the information age.

Having my very patient son James around has been essential for me as I made the painful transition into the digital world, swapping a cement mixer for a computer and a theodolite for an iPhone 5s. I drive him nuts and have lost count of the times he has said 'dad! Just try turning it off and then on again!' I'm actually really starting to get the hang of my emailing machine and now completely understand predictive text ... but really need to read what I have speed-typed before I hit the send button.   I recently sent a text to a guy doing some work for me that said I thought he had 'been making some really tragic decisions'... strategic, I meant strategic! Doh!

Public Speaking! Moi?

... ha ha that is so funny!

The Androcles effect: Androcles faced the most terrifying of man eating Lions ever to enter the ancient Roman Colosseum. But the gentle old fellow found a way of taming the ferocious beast, he simply whispered into its ear and it suddenly abandoned all thought of eating him. Summoned to the royal box, Androcles was asked his secret by the emperor. 'It's this, my lord. I merely told the Lion that as soon as he has finished dinner, he will be asked to say a few words'!

I clearly remember the first month of my property mentorship being told that 'one day some of you guys will be up on stage sharing what you know', and I also remember crossing my arms, my legs, my eyebrows and everything I possessed (negative body language) and thinking 'Ha! No way will you ever get me up on a stage mate!' Little did I know that in less than three years' time my daughter Emily and I would have spoken to more than 2,000 people and spent hundreds of hours in front of audiences from all over the UK!

How did this come about? I'll tell you. By the end of our first year in property we had used up the equity we had taken out of our own property to buy, refurbish and refinance eight 2 and 3 bed properties, and although this was an amazing position to be in, we now felt more than a little stuck as to how to proceed with no money left. Part of our property training had consisted of how to raise joint venture finance but we didn't have the confidence to go down this route and could think of no good reason why anyone would want to lend their money to us so this is why we jumped into the Rent 2 Rent. When we told our mentor (everyone needs a mentor), at first he didn't really pay much attention as it was an unknown quantity and from the outside it probably didn't look like much of an investing strategy. When we mentioned it again six months later he was amazed at how fast we had managed to create a £5k net cash flow, and suggested Emily and I share the information with the other members of the community at the forthcoming weekend gathering. We agreed.

We were told there was really no need to prepare much as it was to be an hour or so informal interview with Emily and I mic'd up and sat on tall stools. We were a little nervous when we realised there would be an audience of sixty but this apprehension was more than cancelled out by our excitement at being able to share this brilliant and fast high cash-flowing strategy. We spent days writing down every conceivable question we may be asked and practicing the answers so it would all seem natural and unrehearsed (!) We were first up on the Sunday morning and were enjoying the banter with the audience so much that the hour just flew past. There was a real buzz in the room and genuine looks of astonishment when we revealed the power of Rent to Rent. The session was winding up and we were a little surprised when it was announced that there was to be a forthcoming one day Rent to Rent course. I can remember wondering who was running it and it was only after 22 places had been sold that I realised that WE were supposed to be running the event! In at the deep end. Eek!

To be perfectly honest we were pleasantly surprised that we quite enjoyed our first taste of stage time and were really up for the challenge of creating a streamlined one day event, especially as we already had an operation

134

manual for the day to day running of our business that we could draw upon and adapt. The first thing we did was to map out how we wanted the day to run, then we amalgamated this into the manual and created some slides for the presentation, I also rummaged around on the internet for some lame property investing jokes, there were lots. Another Einstein quote: *the secret to creativity is knowing how to hide your sources.* This was a slick operation from day one and while I worked on presentation skills, Emily checked and double checked we were factually correct, once again James came to the rescue with all his techi skills and Jane took care of logistics = great teamwork!

The manual: this sounds easy but putting together the highly detailed step by step manual was a mammoth task and a real labour of love. I have been to a few training events over the years and am often more than a little disappointed with the manuals, sometimes really appalled to be frank, so we wanted ours to be different and to stand head and shoulders above the competition. The MLCS manual has now been adopted as the industry standard and many Rent to Rent'ers refer to it as their bible, a real blueprint business in a box. Over the last few years we have spotted or been shown manuals that other training companies are using that look suspiciously like the 1st or 2nd version of ours. Some of the information contained within them is now dangerously out of date as we are constantly updating and improving as the industry evolves. We are now on version nine.

Forty five days later we were all set to go; we had even chosen a 'stage-entry' song - *Bohemian like you* by the Dandy Warhols! (Everyone should have a theme song). We had been given strict instructions not to get off the stools during the presentation, which were now perched on the small stage, this was something I was struggling with by morning break. We found that mine and Emily's style

135

complemented each other perfectly - she would sit quite elegantly and answer any question confidently and with grace. I on the other hand could at times be a little mischievous and had a vast range of terrible jokes to draw on that added a certain something to the day (not exactly sure what!) The day was deemed a great success by all, but Emily and I knew we had a lot of work to do if we were to meet our own exacting standards and saw this as another interesting challenge.

Getting off the stool for good; a famous public speaker once said there are 3 ways to become a better speaker and they are practice, practice and practice, so this is what we did. It was tough at times as were looking after our 50 tenants, running and constantly improving our events and agreeing to speak at pretty much any property event from Manchester to London. I quickly discovered that you get good days and bad days, good crowds and not so good crowds and I also discovered that public speaking is a skill that can be learned like any other, you just had to decide to master it. By our fourth event our 'stool days' were over as we felt safe and secure in ourselves to begin wandering up and down the stage gesticulating like all speakers do, and reserved the tall stools for interviewing our own guests. How times had changed.

Why do people fear speaking in public? A survey once concluded that more people fear public speaking than they fear death, so that would mean they would rather be in the box than reading the eulogy! I find that difficult to believe. I actually don't think it's a fear of speaking at all; it's more a fear of being judged! What if they don't like me, what if I mess up, what if I make a mistake! My way of combating this was to tell myself I had some great information (which I do!) that I wanted to share with people to enable them to make more money and live a better life. I wanted to do a good job, they wanted me to do a good job, and so what

136

was the problem? Judging people is a killer and I really try not to do it.

So Emily and I have now spoken to over 2,000 people including a gig at Wembley Stadium where we really blew the lid off the Rent to Rent strategy and brought it to the masses. And if all goes well by the time you are reading this I will have spoken at the largest property meet in the UK, the Berkshire Property Meet, where I will be sharing how we adapted Rent to Rent, streamlined it and gave it our own flavour. When we were working with our mentor we were under the brand name of *Multi Let Without The Sweat* but this never really sat well with us as it implied there was no work to do, and there is always *some* work to be done! We also didn't really like the word *sweat* in the brand, so when we started to arrange our own events we brainstormed a new name. It was a quick and easy process for us - we worked with *Multi-Lets* and showed people a brilliant *System* to create *Cash-flow* fast and so the Multi-Let Cashflow System was born. The best ideas are usually simple ones.

I quickly realised that what I thought of as humour, others may consider to be sarcasm, which could easily alienate 50% of an audience. What do you think of this; when asked if a rental property must be within walking distance of a railway station I quipped 'everywhere is within walking distance if you have the time'!

The quest of many speakers is to get some audience reaction and this usually starts with asking three 'yes' questions and getting everyone to raise their hands. I was recently listening to a Ted Talk (Google it) about mind control when the speaker said *'All those who believe in telekinesis raise my hand'*. Funny.

Case Study Snapshots

Where are you on the Happiness Scale?

But it's all about results, right? Words are just words and don't mean much unless you turn them into action and turn that action into real money landing in your bank account on a regular basis. At the time of writing there are around 350 people in our MLCS family, many of whom are busy building their Rent to Rent business and are active in the support group, so we all know what is going on in their Multi-Let life. It is hard to track everyone as we are all different and some people attend the training solely to obtain the valuable contracts and then you never hear from them again. Several guys have set up a property literally within days of the training and one gentleman was very excited to tell me he'd set up his first property some 18 months after he attended the course. It was a high payer and he had every reason to be happy. We are all different with lots of stuff going on in our lives so it's whatever works for *you*.

I love it when I get a call or an email from one of the guys to say they have completed another successful deal and I always encourage them to post it in the group to share their accomplishments, which in turn inspires others to more success - it's a virtuous circle. We ask for a *'warts n all'* account of how the deal went from beginning to end as you can learn as much from what goes wrong as what goes right. I don't have space here to dig too deep on case studies but I have asked some of the guys for snapshots of how it's all going for them. As you will see this investment strategy works pretty much all over the UK.

You can check these guys out at

www.mayhemmurderandmultilets.com

These are quick overview examples of a few of the guys who made a decision and decided to do something each and every day to turn that decision into a reality. None of them (to my knowledge) are superhuman or possess any special powers and yet despite all having busy lives they still managed to steadily build a great Rent to Rent high Cash flowing business that will without doubt change the direction of their lives for the better. Many of the guys told me they are using Rent to Rent as a spring board to start purchasing some properties and some of them are doing it all whilst holding down sometimes quite demanding full time jobs. As our community continues to grow and evolve we will continue to support each other, interchange deals, discover and share new and innovative strategies and do joint ventures - this is something we are seeing more and more of as time goes by. I do plan to collect more case studies as I know they are both helpful and inspirational but this will take time. The MLCS guys are sometimes difficult to pin down as once you have a taste for Rent to Rent success you are constantly out there busy looking for more. Also there always seems to be a friendly competition running in the background. Below is the first snapshot case study.

Taking Action Snapshot

Peter Licourinos, Reading

"I've been in property for 15 years and I have no doubt that meeting Francis and Emily Dolley through networking with some friends at a property meet, changed the direction of my life. Since meeting them and attending their course I've now successfully completed 14 let to let deals and I've currently got 3 more that I'm working on. I always aim to be making around £1,000 clear profit per deal. Although I choose to work, I am now in fact financially free and there is no doubt in my mind that it is because of these two people and the training that I attended 12 months ago.

But it's not just about the financial income but also what I have learnt about property and where my company has gone from when I first met them. So, I wouldn't just recommend that you attend the course; I'd say if you are serious about property and making money then you MUST attend the course. I'd happily answer any questions or queries. Happiness scale; an ecstatic ten out of ten".

Tenacity Pays Off

... as nutty as a fruitcake

Setting up the Rent to Rent properties had been a great success but that didn't mean that we wanted to stop *buying* property. Our focus had now completely shifted to Multi Lets for the Turbo-Charged cash flow they produce and if we owned the property we would also benefit from the capital appreciation. We had spotted a brilliant large Victorian 3 storey property some 10 months previously, had made an offer which was accepted and we were due to complete within a month. It was a divorce situation, the property was being sold through an agent and all parties seemed to want to conclude matters as soon as possible, or at least that's the way it first appeared.

We had been to the property several times and got on very well with the lady who lived there, the ex-husband had departed 2 years previous. A month after the offer was accepted the day of completion arrived and all was going very smoothly, in fact on that very same morning I had just had a successful bid on eBay and bought a large and very heavy pine wardrobe and matching chest of drawers. The owner asked if I could collect them straight away and I decided to call the lady to ask if I could drop them off in the house as we were completing in a few hours' time. She was great and said yes, no problem. Then it went a little weird.

On the side of the property was a one bedroom flat. We said we would buy the house subject to planning consent to split the title deed and separate the house from the flat. We were going to refurbish the flat and lease it from the husband for two years. The refurb would cost £4k and we would be able to rent the flat for £535, which would mean a profit for us of almost £9k and then it would be returned to the husband who would benefit from the ongoing rent. All parties and solicitors had agreed on the split but now it seemed that the lady thought something underhand was going on. It actually transpired that a new boyfriend had moved into the house, who was a self-appointed property expert (there are a lot of them about!) and just didn't understand what was going on so he encouraged her to call off the sale! Doh! She still had my wardrobe and chest of drawers. Double Doh!

I tracked down the estranged husband and went to visit him that same afternoon. He was very calm and not at all surprised by the morning's events as it had happened several times before. He said I was in fact the third buyer that she had pulled the plug on. Hmmm, the agent had neglected to mention this! Jane and I got on really well with the gentleman; he pleaded with us to stick to our guns and said he would do whatever it took to get the deal back on track. OK I said, first things first, I wanted my furniture back. He still had a front door key as the house still belonged to him, and he knew the lady of the house worked from 10am to mid-afternoon and so we arranged to meet and retrieve them the next day at 11am. It went like an episode of Mission Impossible and later that day I received the first of very many texts from the said lady. They usually ran to be at least 300mm long on my iPhone and the longest must have been an epic 900mm. They contained many expletives and didn't really make much sense so I stopped reading them.

142

All three solicitors were constantly trying to draw me into a war of letters but I knew how expensive this could work out to be so refused to get involved. It was their problem to sort out not mine and so I got busy with Emily on the Rent to Rent properties. The second completion date came and we all waited with baited breath to see what she would do. There were no surprises as she pulled the plug yet again and demanded I paid for another valuation as she was convinced the property had now increased in value. Her solicitor assured her it had more than likely dropped and she should accept the offer, but no, she was adamant as she had taken professional advice (the boyfriend's!) she paid for the valuation herself, and surprise surprise it came back identical to the last one.

The door into the adjoining flat had now been blocked off and I was finishing off the refurbishment. There was a big hedge running around the property but when I parked up on the day of the proposed 2nd completion I could just about see some notices stuck on all the ground floor windows. This was intriguing so I waited until the lady had disappeared off to work and took a sneaky look. What I saw confirmed that I was really up against it if I ever wanted to complete on this property. There were printed A4 pieces of paper stuck on every ground floor window that exclaimed *'This is the list of people who have p****d me off'*. There was a 'daily' list and a 'permanent' list. There were 3 names on the permanent list including mine! Eek!

Not to be defeated, the team of the ex-husband, myself and our two solicitors set a new completion date and here we go again! We got together with the husband and decided that the only way to go was to force the sale as it was a stipulation of the divorce settlement that the house would be sold and monies shared. It was our plan to turn this property into a seven bed licensed Multi-Let and to do this we had to put in a full planning application and also work with the local authority HMO (House of Multiple

143

Occupancy) officer to make sure the property was up to standard. Emily used her architectural skills to create the drawings and put together the planning application, we used a local company to make sure we were up to date with current building regulations and I met the licensing officer several times so that I could fully understand the licence criteria. I quickly realised that the licensing variations from district to district were huge, even from officer to officer. A big influencing factor seems to be what side of the bed they got out of in the morning and also what they had for breakfast! If I were ever to write a book about HMO licensing it would probably be called '*50 Shades of HMO Grey, with a pinch of salt*'!

The application spluttered to a halt when we discovered a petition had been circulating in the street to stop us getting the planning permission passed. When I found out who was behind it I had to burst out laughing! It was the lady I was trying to buy the house from! This was getting crazier by the second! I decided not to fight it and instead to turn the property into a six bed Multi-Let with an extra communal room as this would not require planning permission. I reconfigured some internal walls so that the room formed part of a mini flat within the property, which meant I could then rent this for a premium.

Twelve months later; it would appear that the neighbour's biggest concern was having six more vehicles trying to park in the street. During the first year of running the property only two tenants owned cars, the others preferred to ride their bikes to work. Some professionals live in shared accommodation to allow them to save money for a deposit on a house or a flat and in fact I have seen that quite a few tenants actually sell their cars when they move in. One of the conditions of the planning was that I built a good solid bicycle store.

Emily and I were so completely absorbed with the Rent to Rent properties and creating a training event (more of

144

that later) that the new completion date arrived before we knew it. I made a quick call to my broker to check all was as it should be, but things had been shifting in the mortgage market and he had some bad news for me ... our mortgage offer had been withdrawn! Ha! I reapplied only to be told that lending criteria had now changed and I was now not eligible for the mortgage, this was fast becoming somewhat farcical. It's always a good idea to have a plan B in place and I wasted no time in contacting the mortgage host I had waiting in the wings. Within a week we were once again all set to go. What else could go wrong?

With all the delay, I had been spending some of our hard earned pennies on setting up the Rent to Rent properties and on living expenses and so now I had to find a new way to finance the deposit to buy this property and to pay for part of the refurb, I needed £50k. At this point I had still not done any joint ventures so first things first; I decided to apply the 3ft rule - that is to tell everyone and anyone who is within 3ft of me! Some people, including me, find it difficult to come right out and ask for money, even if they are offering a brilliant deal for everyone involved, so I used a simple method that I had learned on my property training. I asked the person if they knew anyone who would be interested in making a much better return on their money than they are getting in the bank. Often the response was that they may know someone and that someone often turned out to be themselves! I quickly raised the needed £50k and have in fact now secured over £400k worth of joint ventures without really trying too hard. The rules for joint ventures are changing but the basics remain the same;

- ✓ Start small and build trust
- ✓ Have great communication
- ✓ Get to know each other - are you congruent?
- ✓ See things from their point of view

- ✓ Protect them and their investment
- ✓ Be totally transparent with everything
- ✓ Transfer any money via a solicitor
- ✓ Under promise, over deliver
- ✓ Most importantly, ask your investor this question - what do you want?

While I was doing the refurbishment, I got to know one of the neighbours who had signed the petition, fairly well. Apparently the lady who was selling the house had told everyone I was turning the property into a crack den for delinquent illegal immigrants and I was to be their pimp! He asked me if there was good money in it! This was a man who adamantly refused to accept his hearing was completely shot even though his every sentence began with 'Can you repeat that please'? He was convinced the Mexican Government just announced a 'war on rugs'! This reminded me of the confusion a few years ago when George Bush Jnr. announced 'a war on 'tourism'!

I decided to have an open day at the house to show friends and colleagues what I had been up to and perhaps get them interested in investing in future projects. This was also the day I found out about a damp problem that had arisen in the flat next door. I didn't know it at the time but the gentleman who had rented it four months previously never turned the heating on (couldn't afford to), never opened a window (too cold), turned off the bathroom extraction fan (too noisy) and tried to dry all his soaking wet clothes on the radiators (it's raining outside). This is an absolutely perfect breeding ground for damp and mould and it just so happened that his somewhat psychotic mother was visiting that very same day!

Even though the walls were quite thick, the distinctive chinking of champagne glasses and raucous laughter could apparently be heard quite clearly and this enraged the mother! Her son later told me that he pleaded with his mother not to speak to me until he had first but she was having none of it and marched right into my house to tell the world what a dreadful landlord I was for allowing her poor son to live in these conditions. My assurances that I would deal with it first thing in the morning and that it couldn't be that bad as it was all brand spanking new four months previous not only fell on deaf ears but seemed to enrage her more and she made a grab for my throat!

Once again I had that feeling that this was not happening to me, I guess it's like those out of body experiences that you sometimes read about. My friends were fast to respond and quickly ushered her out of the door but she did not leave willingly and continued to hammer her tiny clawed fists on the door like an angry woodpecker, until the son came to retrieve her. I shrugged and said 'more champagne anyone' - there is always time amid the chaos for another glass of champagne!

The tenant asked if he could give a week's notice and as our relationship had completely broken down I agreed to release him from his obligations as soon as we found a suitable replacement. I can never understand landlords who hold tenants to their contract when both sides are unhappy, much better to move on. Before the week was up I had installed a special £400 fan, got the damp cleaned and repainted and added a section to our tenants 'Guide to Living' about avoiding damp and moisture, which I thought would have been common sense but apparently common sense is in short supply these days!

Would you have walked away from this deal? The flat made me a good chunk of money before we handed it back and the licensed HMO will continue to make a healthy deposit in my account for the foreseeable future. Some of the single let properties had initially been 'sold' to someone else before they came back to me. Tenacity is an important character trait in the world of property investing.

Taking Action Snapshot

Kathryn Slack, Nottingham

"I attended the MLCS course in deepest but not darkest, Somerset. I acquired my first property soon after the course and now have 7 in my portfolio. My net cash flow is currently just over £4,000 per month. I aim to increase the portfolio to a total of 20 over the next 18 months. Some of the properties had just been refurbished so when I took them on, they still had that lovely smell of fresh paint! Our other properties have come from agents with distressed landlords!

Prior to attending the MLCS course, I was working for a multi-national company as a Project Manager. My customers are household names including Kellogg, Cadbury and IKEA. I still work for this company but the speed that my Rent to Rent business is growing means I will be able to replace my salary - I plan to clear some personal debt and recoup my initial investment into the business before I quit the day job, which will be very soon.

If you were to ask me where I am on the 'happiness' scale, it has to be a 10 out of 10! This is a fantastic business. I get great support from the MCLS team and the Facebook group and everyone spurs everyone on so it feels like a family. It is a brilliant course with a very informative manual you can review regularly after the training. There are also oodles of documents you can use which mean we didn't need to reinvent the wheel I would really recommend and strongly urge you to join the training programme. It's fantastic, just do it!"

The Multi-Let Cashflow System

... Turbo-charging your cash flow

Bicycles are a brilliant invention but I believe they can be improved a little, so I have designed a different shaped wheel. I haven't tested it yet but I have spent a lot of money on the new design and many hours choosing the perfect tyre colour.

How crazy does that sound?

I actually get to hear that quite regularly. I often meet guys who say they don't need any training as all you need to do is rent a property and then sublet the rooms and that's really simple. I say OK and sincerely wish them good luck. Then I get some guys wanting to pick my brains at events, on the phone, by emails - they pick and pick and pick probably thinking, as I used to, that you can get what you want for free and they will get enough information to set up their business. I am always happy to give an overview of our system and once again I wish them good luck. Maybe they get it all rolling and secure some high cash flowing properties or maybe, and I think this is most likely, they struggle to even get started and then continue on searching for more free information but are never quite able to connect all the pieces of the jigsaw.

Often months later I may get calls and emails from those same guys who want to know why the agents are

149

shunning them or who have run into difficulties with the contracts they have downloaded from an Hungarian Estate Agent's website! What they are doing is trying to create their own system. You wouldn't really try to reinvent the bike (would you?) so why try to reinvent a system that has been proven to work time and time again by everyone from established investors to a complete novice? Just copy it. Add your own special flavour and your own distinctive style by all means, but just copy and stick to the system.

I have a confession.

I absolutely (and that's a word I don't often use!) knew that property investing was the right industry to get into; I had seen the evidence all around me for many years and had no doubt it would create the long term stability for me and my family that I craved. In fact as a builder I had been helping many people build their mini property empires over the years, all the time scared to take those first steps and probably whinging to all and sundry about the raw deal I was getting and how I was smarter than them and deserved a better life and ... baaaahaaa! The truth was, that by doing nothing, not only was I gambling the future financial security of my family, I was also resigning us all to a good life. What's wrong with that you might ask? Well I think that the only thing that stopping most people from having a great life, is a good life! If your life is mostly trucking along nicely, why upset the apple cart and put yourself in that uncomfortable position of being outside of your comfort zone? Let's just pretend everything is hunky dory and carry on, I'm sure the Government will look after us. I did this for ten years. Ten years! I was so busy worrying about the price of getting some professional training that I failed to count the cost of not doing it. If I had started ten years earlier where would I be now? But no point in looking back, let's keep moving forward, eh?

So I have experienced exactly the same emotions that stop a lot of people from taking action and for many years

150

doubted all the evidence that was there for all to see, before I *finally* took a deep breath and decided to take the plunge. Making a decision and committing yourself totally to something is exhilarating, it's like leaping out of an aeroplane! Some trainers will tell you to 'jump, and grow your wings on the way down'! Hmmmm. I'm not so sure, I agree - my mantra has always been to 'get all your ducks in a row' and that's not to suffer from analysis paralysis but to make a plan of action and move forward at a pace each and every day. (Those Slight Edge principles again)

MLCS: Emily and I wanted to make our training days different than the others out there. Number one, we wanted to massively over-deliver and surprise attendees both on the day and most importantly after they have completed the training - more of that in a moment. Number two, we wanted our training to be results based and whilst we cannot call around to everyone's house banging on doors and insisting they take action, we do our utmost to constantly encourage and inspire on-line. Number three, we wanted to create a community or as Seth Godin would say, a Tribe, of likeminded and supportive people who would in turn inspire others with their results and therefore the whole thing would eventually start to self-perpetuate.

So we make the events fun and vary the styles of learning throughout the day, and I can honestly say no one has ever fallen asleep yet, not even the lady who flew in from New Zealand the night before or the gentleman who came directly to our training from Iraq! Maybe they both flew first class? I believe that a major flaw with a lot of the trainings out there is as soon as they are over and you walk out the door you are on your own! I started thinking about this and came to the conclusion that it is more than a little arrogant of anyone to think that they can talk to you about a subject for eight hours (often much less) and that you will get EVERYTHING you need! It is pretty common and almost customary for most people to feel a little overwhelmed when they have completed a new training session and are assimilating all the information. What normally happens next is that a whole host of new questions will spring to mind and they make a list, and they come up with even more questions and add to the list. Then what do they do? Well, they struggle on slowly and if they are lucky they will fail their way forward to success. Nothing wrong with this but it's akin to a three legged donkey trying to climb up a ladder with an anvil tied to its tail.

Do we guarantee success after attending one of our events? A-b-s-o-l-u-t-e-l-y ... not! We give you the best information with the best support system available but at the end of the day it's *you* that has to take action. Business has always had inherent risks and a lot of small businesses fail in their first year but getting the correct education reduces that risk substantially and you will have a chance of success if you start with the right training. Personal development is good but business development is also crucial, as is the ability to raise finance - there is 30 billion dollars circulating the globe and you need to channel some of that money your way!

So we decided we would be different and offer everyone who has completed our event lifetime support via a Facebook support group. Yes you read that right - not a month's *limited* access or three months *reasonable* email support, but welcome everyone into the MLCS family lifetime support community, and to use an Americanism, we think that is pretty goddamn awesome! This was extremely time consuming for us in the beginning but as the community has grown, people have gained great experience and become more proficient and it has become self-sufficient. I've just had a thought; we have built such a great community that even if I was no longer around, the MLCS family could now carry on without me (to that sad theme tune from Titanic, *'I will go on'*, sniff, sniff!).

152

Being Back on the Chain Gang

... and why balloon chasing can be most discombobulating!

One of my best friends once gave me a tin plaque for a birthday that read 'Welcome to the Sarcasm Society ... *like we need your support!*' I was recently accused (?) of being sarcastic when I referred to someone as a 'balloon chaser'. What I meant was that they had set up their property business so that they were forever running this way and then that way and then over here and then back over there, in fact whichever way the wind blew them! Phew I was getting exhausted just talking to them. If they were not suffering from it already, they were heading for a severe case of overwhelm.

Feeling overwhelmed is a common problem in most rapidly growing small businesses and especially in the case of first time entrepreneurs who grab hold of every job with vigour, excitement and enthusiasm. How do I know this? How do you think? I was no different - if you hit the ground running in a new industry you are bound to make mistakes and drop a few balls. The real question is how fast do you recover from mistakes and what do learn from them. This is another reason to get some proper training - mistakes can be time consuming, frustrating and expensive!

Ask any experienced entrepreneur and they will tell you to outsource a long time before you need to, to avoid becoming overwhelmed. There are two problems with this:

1. Money is often an issue when starting out and most people would rather spend money on upgrading furniture than a virtual assistant; and

2. When you are starting out you are not really sure what it is exactly that you need to outsource! I guess it's another case of which came first - the chicken or the egg? All the time you are creating an all-consuming job that was supposed to free you from your last job!

Emily and I like to give 100% at all times - to our tenants, to event delegates, to the MLCS community, and we were struggling. So we came to a major decision that in hindsight was long overdue. I always said that I loved the interaction with tenants and this was true, tenants are (mostly) part of the human race after all, and it is in my nature to be friendly and interested in other people. As the Rent to Rent and events businesses started to grow I felt like I was getting pulled in too many different directions and actually started to scowl at the phone whenever a tenant called with another minor issue (missing sausages, fridge light not working). So Emily and I made a decision to bring in a property manager as we both felt that our time would be better spent elsewhere - Emily on growing the Rent to Rent portfolio and mine working on growing the training events business. But we didn't really want to take a hit on the money the properties were bringing in to pay for that manager; we're just greedy I guess!

We not only succeeded in eventually finding and employing a brilliant property manager (after a few false starts) but we also made more money in the process by implementing some new and really quite simple systems. In fact the whole process has been fantastic for us on so many levels that I would highly recommend that even if you are not ready yet, you get some systems in place now to prepare for the day. We go through the whole process of how we found and employed our manager, step by step in our new Advanced Training programme. So we have the solid foundational MLCS *'How to set up a high Cashflowing property'* training day which includes the lifetime support community and now we have the more advanced MLCS E.D.G.E. training to Turbo-Charge your success from one property ... to infinity and beyond (sorry got carried away there as watched *Toy Story 3* last night!).

This is an extra guidance and coaching programme for those who want big results and fast. It meant analysing every detail of what we had achieved to date and working with a small team from the MLCS family to test drive the new system to see if it worked. It did! It also meant that we had to create a brand new manual with details of all the cutting edge strategies, so another labour of love. This manual was then scrutinised and every component evaluated by the team, and when all the manuals had been returned to us they were all amalgamated and edited into the final copy. We also designed some new and cool branding, put together a new training day with specialised speakers and set up a membership site amongst other things.

As well as this, we are currently working on creating the MLCS home-study course and will be running some live 'Working with Estate Agents' training days, which will also be turned into a home-study course.

This is a huge amount of work that will help to grow our training business and enhance the MLCS community, and was only possible by implementing the art of leverage and by outsourcing much of the work. If Emily and I had continued to juggle everything as we were, we would have just become better at giving a worse service to everyone and destroyed any credibility we may have had! So leverage = get more work done to a better standard.

We are now building little teams for all the different areas of our lives and businesses. If only I could find someone to iron my shirts to my exacting standards!

As we saw how well this whole process unfolded, the idea of leveraging everything became very appealing, so we looked at every task we did and whether we could outsource it. In fact, I now have Post It notes stuck to one side of my computer that say *'Outsource, Manage, Automate, Do!'* This acts as a constant reminder to focus on money making tasks first and not get caught up with trivial jobs that can easily be outsourced. After all, are you in business to make money or just tell your friends what a busy busy life you have? This is so important and I really can't emphasise it enough.

Emily was recently writing an article where she said *'I used to organise my life around my work but now it's the other way around'*. This was great to hear and really it's the way we should all be living our lives. She was able to do this by first examining what she actually needed in her life and stripped away anything else. We are only on this planet for a short time so why spend it chasing money just to enable you to pay more bills, much better to live lightly and streamline your life to what you actually *need*. You could start by Google'ing Maslow's Hierarchy of Needs, where he examines what motivates us to do the things we do. He determined that we all have Physiological, Safety, Belongingness and Love, Esteem and Self-Actualization needs. He reasons the need for living a balanced life, the need for constant improvement and the desire to realise your full potential and to be whatever you *'can'* be. This is thought provoking and a whole huge subject of its own.

Taking Action Snapshot

Fazel Ullah, London

"I was already a full-time property Investor in South London, specializing in Multi-Lets and Buy To Lets when I attended Francis and Emily's event on June 1st 2013. I then spent June and July getting my systems ready, dealing with all set up tasks and laying the foundations. I got started officially with my first two properties in August.

I had the desire to accelerate my growth in property and found Rent to Rent to be an incredible way to maximize Cash-flow with such small amounts of cash input, and with the profit being anything between £600 and £1,000, I feel it is a no brainer.

I am really enjoying this new lifestyle very much. This strategy has boosted my cash-flow big-time to a net income of £5,000 per month! My intermediate goal is to secure one property per month - so 12 properties each year. I also have a bigger plan; my end goal is to grow the business to 50 properties by 2018 and I am already on track and on target. I will then start using the funds generated to buy properties using my own cash.

The follow up support from Francis, Emily and the community has been absolutely amazing and crucial to my success. All my questions get answered very quickly, helping me accelerate my growth and create Massive Cash-flow from this R2R Strategy. I would thoroughly recommend that anyone who is hungry to create cash-flow through property with little investment join us, as the returns are amazing.

12 out of 10 for happiness!
Stay blessed, Love, Health and happiness".

The Tip of the Iceberg

... and the great leap forward

Eddie Cantor was a Broadway star of the 1930's and is the first person accredited with saying 'It takes 20 years to become an overnight success'! I can't help but think of Eddie every time I hear the phrase 'new craze' or 'get rich quick' when applied to Rent to Rent, as it too has been around for at least 20 years. What has recently happened is that instead of hanging around at the back of the theatre it has been shoved up on the stage for all to see and scrutinise.

After Emily and I did our talk at the largest property event in the UK - the Property Super Conference in Wembley Stadium, in front of 1,000 investors, we were approached by many experienced guys saying that they wish we hadn't done it. It was not that they thought there was anything wrong with what we had said, quite the contrary, it's just that we had let the cat out of the bag and they were afraid that now *everyone* was going to be doing it. At the after dinner party, one high profile guy kept insisting in a booming loud voice that we 'compromise', but we never quite got to the bottom of what exactly he wanted us to compromise.

Some of these high profile guys, including established letting and estate agents, had been very quietly running successful Rent to Rent businesses on the side for many years, they had pretty much cornered their local market and were making an absolute killing! I now know that this is the mere tip of the iceberg, with most people going about it very quietly and not publicising the fact for fear of criticism. But, thanks to Emily and me, the cat was now indeed well and truly out of the bag! Meeow.

The feedback from the Wembley talk was mixed, as Rent to Rent really seems to stir the emotions of some people like no other strategy. Mostly from people who didn't believe the numbers and who started each sentence with an *'I've been investing for 20 years and I've never ...'*, but the uptake was massive and a few weeks later we ran the first of a series of MLCS training events for 60 people. We were also asked to speak at various networking events up and down the country; we wrote many articles for property related magazines and started to run a series of big bright adverts to promote our forthcoming events. We did some webinars and were interviewed several times for radio and podcasts, so I guess you could say we were raising the Rent to Rent profile and bringing it to the masses!

As time went by I could see that this actually seemed to really annoy some of the more established investors who seemed to think that we should desist from running courses and the information should be kept under wraps for their secret club. It was getting like an episode of *Kung Foo and Sacred Fist Society!* On the other hand, I totally understand how tough life can be at times and if I have information that I think will be of benefit, I feel compelled to share it. It's that attitude of abundance that I totally buy into and that I truly believe that the more you give the more you get in return ... well, most of the time!

A consequence of running events is that some people will attend to get all the valuable contracts, the documentation, the forms, the manual and everything else we provide and then start running their own events. When this first happened the person in question had promotional pictures taken holding our manual - all they had changed was the name and contact details! We had a few words and were a little miffed at first but then thought, hey ho it's a kind of flattery ... I guess. We can now count five people who have attended our training and are now running their own events albeit with somewhat outdated versions of our manual as the industry moves forward at a pace, especially the legal aspect. We decided to shrug it off and instead keep striving on for better systems that actually work and better results. As a consequence we have attracted a better quality of customer which has in turn enhanced the MLCS support group. Some of these guys we really admire and love so instead of wasting energy competing with each other we have in fact been moving towards working together with one to one coaching sessions and honing the finer points of Rent to Rent. It's a virtuous circle and preferable to compromise, which is after all an agreement between two sides to do what both agree is wrong!

Lower the Life Boat, I'm in!

... and full speed ahead!

You may have been misfortunate enough to have stumbled upon a trashy Rent to Rent article that was published in a national newspaper, which was then rehashed by various on and off-line 'reporters' too lazy to do their own research. The ridiculous suppositions contained therein then spilled over onto several property forums, where a certain contingent of posters who for reasons unknown began jumping up and down, slapping their thighs and howling at the moon! This minority seem to be vehemently opposed on even a molecular level, not only to Rent to Rent but seemingly to property trainings in any way shape or form!

I remember one such post referring to anyone who ran trainings as *snake oil salesmen*, and even (in a derogatory fashion) Guru's! Shock horror. I ask you, don't they know we have feelings too? But for every Yin there is a Yang and I realise this is a really small (but unrelenting) group of individuals who are very vocal and make sure we all get to hear their opinions.

A while ago I was at a dinner party in a big old country house in the depths of Somerset when I found myself seated beside an elderly gentleman. We got chatting and eventually the inevitable 'what do you do for a living' came up. He was a retired barrister and it soon became apparent that he had been around the block a few times and seen and done most things in his long and colourful career. I explained what I did and also mentioned the unwarranted negativity Rent to Rent had been attracting at that time from the mainstream press and the constant and somewhat repetitive bombardment from a handful of people on their self-appointed anti Rent to Rent crusade. His insight and advice was brilliant.

The meal was just about over and everyone had moved to the next room where a huge log fire was burning. We two remained in the large dining room where he sat back in his leather club chair sipping at his brandy and listening intently.

After I had concluded my tale he said 'Francis, any twit can find problems; it's easy, what does take a little more intelligence and enterprise is to find answers to those problems, and there is always an answer. There is nothing more annoying than people who dish out criticism like they're going to win a prize for it. The only sure fire way to avoid criticism in this life my boy (I didn't mind him calling me that), is by saying nothing, doing nothing and being nothing! But you can rest assured Francis that whatever you do in life an 'energy' will spring up to oppose you. It's only natural; consider history and the many battles won and lost, big and small. What you must do my dear boy is to turn that criticism into your own energy!'

I told him I didn't understand what he meant, and so he asked me if I jumped in with all guns blazing whenever anyone made disparaging remarks aimed at me or the Rent to Rent system. I said I sometimes did and made my case for the defence by insisting it was only a natural reaction. He didn't disagree but gave me some great counsel. He said; "Next time it happens don't be such an eager beaver and instead of bounding in, sit back and ask your antagonists to explain further the issue. Make sure they give you an in-depth, full, considered reply and identify

162

each and every one of the flaws in your proposal. You may then be able to wheedle out a few solutions before your adversary realises what you are doing. Try it on a few of the scoundrels to make sure you are fully armed with all their condemnations and misguided judgements."

It dawned on me where he was going with this and I smiled. He smiled back and said he had been using this technique in court for many years to great effect. I smiled some more.

"You must then enter into a time of research and make sure you not only get an answer to every miniscule detail of even the most trivial of criticisms, but you must also absorb it and internalise it. So you see that your critics have become an important part of your team in helping you to identify the flaws and instead of holding you back or stopping you, they have in fact propelled you forward like greased lightning! Not only that but they work for you for free!"

Brilliant, this was just brilliant and made me realise I had been looking at a lot of things in an upside down kind of way; life would never be the same again. But it was getting late, the barrister's wife was discretely tapping her watch, Jane was stifling a yawn and the host was putting the milk bottles and the cat out. As we walked to the door he said one more thing; 'There could be an altogether divergent and quite common reason for your adversary's reaction. Is it possible that they want to protect their position by pulling the ladder up so that no one else can ascend to the lofty heights of their privileged position? A case of I'm all right jack!' As I bade him goodnight I considered this. I remembered a logo form a charity I had liked - one hand raised to pull yourself up and the other lowered to help the person below you, an attitude of abundance, sadly not everyone shares that same attitude.

Criticism in any shape or form can be very upsetting and it is a natural reaction to want to stalwartly defend your position. I have at times spent a good hour crafting a wordy and clever reply to a person that dared take an opposing view to me (don't deny it, you've done it too!). But lately have seen the folly in this. There is nothing wrong with a good debate but there is little point in wasting your time attempting to convert someone who is totally unwilling to even consider your point of view. I once knew a person who could ruin any dinner party - he would never change his mind and would never change the subject!

Realising that what other people thought of me was really none of my business was quite liberating. It is stifling in the extreme to allow yourself to be constantly constrained by the thoughts, words and beliefs of other people that may barely even know you. Everyone may have an opinion of you, some will think you're brilliant and some will think you're stupid (but in actual fact most people are tuned into WIIFM) but should you really allow that to be a major contributing factor in you deciding how you live your life?

Criticism often says more about the person dishing it out than the person on the receiving end. It is far better to learn to disengage and relinquish the opinions of others and stay focused on what you are trying to achieve. Know why you are here and where your path lies. Rudyard Kipling says it better than I ever could in his poem 'If'. If you are struggling with low self-esteem due to the impositions of others I would print this poem, laminate it and put it in your hand/man bag!

Taking Action Snapshot

Tracey Stewart, Leicester

"I'm an investor based in Leicester and first got into property back in 2003 when I bought my first buy to let property. I dabbled a bit here and there and went on to acquire a couple more but never really got anywhere with it. I tried lease options and deal packaging but they really weren't for me. In March 2013 I heard about the Francis Dolley course the Multi Let Cashflow System and decided to take the plunge and go on the course. 6 weeks later I acquired my first rent to rent property and since then I have gone on to take on another 6 properties, so 7 in total in the portfolio and building. On the course we learnt all about the mindset, dealing with agents, landlords, managing HMO's - all completely new territory for me. A huge benefit of the course is a fantastic Facebook group with a big community which offers a lifetime of support and is there for you every step of the way.

For the next couple of months my intention is to continue growing it and then I am going on to attend the MLCS advanced training programme to create a real business, so I can really take it to new heights. I would highly recommend this course, it's fantastic, and it covers everything you need. It's a real business in a box - all you have to do is Take Action! So go for it and sign up.

Happiness scale; ten out of ten!"

My Zipper's Stuck!

... as the pantomime horse backed

into the scenery

Would you like to take a peek behind the curtain of running events?

Running an event is easy; you just book a room, stick a few posts on Facebook and wait for everyone to turn up, right? Ummm, wrong. Running a good event can be all consuming and was once accurately described as trying to blow up an airbed with a hole in the other end - you are continually huffing and puffing so that it seems like an endless and thankless job. In fact there was a time after one particular eventful event when the build-up had been so completely manic for one reason or another, that I was seriously considering quitting for good. It was getting too much like the fidgety stressful hard work that I had wanted to escape from.

There are many elements to running an event; first deciding you have a market, creating good course content, formulating this into a manual, possibly a workbook and a power-point presentation. You will need to find a supplier to print the manual as cheaply as possible whilst retaining top quality. You will have to consider the style and accessibility of the venue, the day delegate rate, the layout of the room, the crew and their roles on the day, name badges, the sound system, the standard of food and refreshments throughout the day. You will have to decide how you will market the event; this will have to constantly evolve and you will have to be constantly looking for new means to fill the rooms. (This is where the air bed analogy comes in). You may be offered joint venture opportunities and you will have to decide which ones will be of benefit to you and which ones will just drain your energy. You will have to decide on a payment system and possibly register for VAT. To ensure you remain relevant as the market changes, you will need to constantly update the course content and ensure all crew members are up to speed.

Oh and let's not forget to keep the room exactly the perfect temperature at all times for all 40 strangers in the room! What would you say was the optimum temperature?

All of this is possible if you have the time, the resources and most of all the drive and energy. I am very fortunate to have around me people who feel as passionate about delivering the best top notch A1 training as I do. But sometimes things don't go to plan.

We have turned up at venues to find no sound system which resulted in me almost losing my voice by the end of the day. No curtains at a venue, which meant the afternoon sun completely obliterated the screen for an hour. (I had to describe contents of the slides). We picked up the manuals the day before one event only to find every other page was complete gobbledygook - the printer only checked the first copy! The day before a January event a monsoon hit the UK followed by a great British freeze and stayed until the day after the event (only one person didn't make it - I love the great British spirit of refusing to accept defeat!) One venue we booked had no air conditioning but we were assured this was no problem as we could open the 3 large French doors. This created another problem as the venue was on a hill and vehicles would noisily rev their engines which resulted in me having to shout - and this was the venue with no sound system!

But the biggest 'disaster' for me was the venue with the modern stone-bowl style basins in the bathroom. We have a very talented crew who now do mini presentations of their own which is great as it gives me a chance to run to the loo if I have been drinking too many mugs of green tea. One of the presentations was quite short so I was in a hurry to get back and in my haste turned the modern and initially unfathomable basin tap on full blast. Water gushed out, circumnavigated the bowl and took flight, splashing all over my light coloured trousers! Argghhh, disaster! I instantly knew what I had to do - I quickly grabbed a chair from the hallway and quietly returned to the WC where I stood on said chair and directed the hand-drier towards my lower regions as I rubbed furiously with paper towels. Thankfully no one entered the bathroom and it didn't take long to dry out. Unfortunately with all the excitement I had overlooked closing my zipper and all that vigorous swiping with the handtowels had now rammed my zipper down as far as it would go. Jammed solid! Leaving my shirt un-tucked to hide my shame, I gingerly skipped over in a mild panic to the door where the crew were sitting and beckoned to Jane for assistance, she followed me giggling back to the bathroom where she knelt down and tried to free the rogue zipper. It took several minutes of tugging and grunting with me stood hands on hips encouraging her to be quick! Just as she managed it the bathroom door opened and an older gentleman walked in, he looked aghast, said 'oh very sorry' and hurriedly left again! I later discovered he was on a speed awareness course in another room. I sniggered my way back to the training room while Jane shook her head in disbelief at the trouble I get her into. Lesson learnt; more haste, less speed! It's all in the police report.

As the training business grew we have had to learn many new skills such as hosting webinars, list building, how to set up and use auto responders, how to set up a video studio, how to edit the videos and this in turn has meant that we have had to constantly upgrade just about everything. Like all things in life, sometimes it all goes well and sometimes things don't go quite so well. We still get the occasional disaster. I always say that if you can smile when everything around you is going wrong, you have probably already thought of someone to blame it on. But if that is not possible then you need to extract yourself from the situation as quickly as possible and remove any evidence that you were ever there in the first place! HeHe! Joking aside, as you grow and push the boundaries things will always go wrong from time to time but the real test is how fast you recover and learn from your mistakes. I am very fortunate to have a smart supportive family and have built a brilliant team around me. The optimal room temperature is 19 degrees.

Health Creation

... and accidental eating

What do wealthy people make for lunch? ... Reservations!

This is a cheeky little, but important chapter on health. We often hear the term wealth creation with a focus on making and accumulating money, but something that I believe must work alongside this is 'health creation'. The Slight Edge principle is at work here also and if it's not working for you it's working against you, there is no standing still. I have a good friend who was determined to lose the weight he been steadfastly collecting over the years and because he persevered really hard with his diet all week he would 'reward' himself at the weekends with a big fry-up. I asked him why he thought of this as a reward as I would think of this as a punishment and it would go a long way to undo all that hard work he had done during the week. He never answered; I think the thought of never having another overloaded plate of greasy food that would 'set him up for the day' was just too painful to contemplate, though probably not as painful as a mild heart attack in the not too distant future!

Personally I think it is much better to adopt a lifestyle of healthy eating and healthy living than to be constantly dieting and awarding yourself treats for doing well. I really liked a quote by Zig Zigler (in his dry Texan drawl) *'I don't ever recall eating anything by accident'*, and this made me very conscious of what I was putting in my mouth. It's not easy to change the habits of a lifetime and to question ingrained beliefs so I decided to start by applying the 80-20 principle. I would be good, exercise and eat well 80% of the time until this became the new 'norm', then the last 20% would just fall into place which it did very quickly. Do I stick to this new regime at all times? No of course not, I am only human after all, but the more I keep to it and correct my little indiscrepancies the easier it gets.

Over the years I have seen a slight deterioration in people's health all around me and I have especially seen more overweight people and people with general health issues. I have recently been reading and listening to food/health books and have come to the conclusion that we are not really designed to eat meat; our digestive system is just not designed to cope with it. Neither should we be consuming dairy, in fact we are the only animal on the planet that continues to drink milk after we have been weaned from our mothers. Not only that but we get that milk from a completely different species! I now only drink Almond milk.

Years ago when I developed an intolerance to wheat and started spending hours loitering in supermarkets reading the ingredients on everything, I soon realised that there are very few 'natural' foods after you have passed through the fruit and veg section, in fact it's a chemical sh*t-storm out there! I didn't know what most of the additives were and so decided I would no longer put things I did not recognise into my body! You can't go wrong with fruit and veg ... can you? Pesticide is a nasty word and often used by farmers to increase their crops (profits), so that meant trusting the supermarkets to tell the truth, buying only organic or growing my own ... and I don't have green fingers! In Somerset we are lucky enough to have organic vegetables delivered to your door, these are more expensive but then what price do you place on the wellbeing of that highly complex Trillion Dollar machine that you carry your brain around in? At a very basic level it is a good idea to question anything that has 'ingredients' and eat more 'whole' foods.

The food and supermarket industry is big business and we mustn't forget that their primary concern is being profitable. This realization has made me want to question everything that may have an adverse effect on my health from the food I eat, the toothpaste and shampoo I use and even how often I use my mobile phone. We should not accept what we are being told by people who stand to make vast profits by selling us their products. Your new mantra - question everything and have a vegetable smoothie for breakfast. After just two weeks of changing to a vegetable smoothie, if I don't have one I now really miss, even crave one. If you are interested I make the smoothies from whatever vegetables I have to hand and it usually contains a whole cucumber, celery, green pepper, curly kale, a few bits of fruit especially a mango and a splash of almond milk.

From a business point of view, if you take care of yourself, eat well and exercise regularly you will feel more vital and energised and therefore get more done and possibly make more money. It's more of a virtuous circle as opposed to the bad food/no exercise vicious circle. Who knows you might even meet a joint venture partner at the gym? I used to play five-a-side football which is a terrific way to stay fit but had to stop due to a recurring back injury and it was only when I decided to take up running that I realised the one thing harder than getting in shape is getting back into shape!

I have always struggled with keeping up gym memberships for one reason or another and so decided to buy a good quality professional running machine from eBay and managed to get one for the bargain price of £400, a sixth of its true value. I now run 5k every other day but this wasn't easy in the beginning as due to the back problem every step I took was agony. But I was determined. So I bought a transcutaneous electrical nerve stimulation unit. A what!! It's also known as a TENS machine. This is a small portable, battery-operated device about the size of a mobile phone. The unit is attached by wires to eight sticky pads which I stuck to my back on either side of my spine. Electrical pulses were then transmitted which dulled the pain enough for me to continue running and after a few painstaking months I was able to pack it away back in its box. Most people go running with iPods or iPhones, I had a TENS machine! It is actually very easy to adjust your diet and begin to regularly exercise, but then it's just as easy not too. I suppose the moral here is do not accept defeat - decide to do something and find a way, oh and take care of yourself because the chances are no one else will!

Keeping fit can be a dangerous business. I ordered a public speaking audio from America and early one morning several weeks later the postman pushed it though my door just as I was heading for my running machine. I was excited to get it and so took a detour and quickly burnt it onto iTunes and loaded it onto my iPhone so that I could listen to it as I was running. That day I was feeling really energised and so turned the running machine up a notch or two. The audio was great, better than I had expected but I had forgotten to disengage the random play button, so at the end of the first track I was suddenly listening to Brian Tracy encouraging me to 'eat the frog'! I didn't want to eat a frog at that particular moment and so started grappling with the iPhone that was strapped to my arm. In my frustration I inadvertently placed one foot on the side bar which remained there as my other foot was snatched out from under me by the relentless running track. Have you ever experienced time slowing down? This is what happened in the next half a second as I was pitched onto the

173

speeding track in slow motion and slammed into the solid wall behind me. I did as most men would do, I jumped up and looked around me to make sure no one had seen and then I carried on running, now with a slight sideways gait! I later discover I was missing skin from various parts of my body. Ouch! When I relate this story to people who exercise they look fearful and show great concern, however when I relate it to non-exercisers they roll around the floor laughing and suggest perhaps it might to time to give up all this tom-foolery! Crabs!

> *My favourite foodie joke: Vegetarian - it's an old Indian word that means 'lousy hunter'...*

OK, one last little observation on the matter of health. I have a larger than life (in every way!) friend who lives not far from me and is more than a little fanatical about his car, which is an *Audi R8 Spyder* with a starting price of over £100k (I Googled it!) It's not for me to say if he can afford to drive this car but it is the most expensive of his possessions by far (he rents his house). He spends at least every Sunday out in the street slowly washing, even lovingly caressing this red shiny gas guzzler with a moist soapy sponge. He also makes a habit of eating at either the American Embassy (*McDonalds*) or a greasy burger all-you-can-eat joint in a town where I have some investment properties (I really don't understand the concept of those 'all you can eat' restaurants). I often see him jovially and enthusiastically devouring enough food to feed the population of a small country while sat at a window seat eyeing the love of his life, which is usually parked right outside. I seriously think the human body is miracle of engineering that too many people take for granted. So I have two questions; 1. His car may have cost £100k but what value is he putting on his own health and quality of his life? 2. Will he leave his car to me when his body gives

174

up the ghost? Health can be like sand in an hour glass, it keeps silently slipping away until it's just too late. Take care of yourself.

Taking Action Snapshot

Katrina Jones, York

"My area is York. I did the MLCS training and I got started in 2013. It was 10am on 1st July to be exact lol. My big reason ... I love my freedom and didn't want to be tied down to a 9-5 job! I wanted to find my real passion in life and have the time and money to do that instead :-) My current net cash flow is just over £4k.

Happiness scale out of 10 = 11!!!!!!!"

In fact I am so ridiculously grateful that I can't really put it into words. The feeling of being in total control of my own destiny is overwhelming and incredible. Of course I have Francis and MLCS to thank 100% for this amazing feeling xxx THANK YOU! xxx No more wishing that there was one more day of the weekend! This training has given me so much confidence in so many ways."

Katrina Jones, UK Crusader at League of Extraordinary Women and Director at Kendell Bailey www.katrina-jones.com.

Building a Business

... a time to stop and regroup

The truth is, sales is all about making peoples' lives better.

So you have completed some training, decided to take action and set up a few Rent to Rent properties which are full and making you money. It's been a steep learning curve, you have had some brilliant highs and a few hard lessons along the way but are totally convinced you have made the right decision and are now thinking about the future and growing this into a real business. As one MLCS delegate said 'I am so ridiculously grateful to be at last in control of my own destiny'. This is exactly how Emily and I feel. We count our blessings each and every day for discovering this system and sometimes sit down together and say out loud all the things we are grateful for. Like me, you may at first consider this to be some hocus pocus mumbo jumbo from the world of Tony Robbins *(I can do it, I know I can do it!)* and feel a little silly. But it does help me to feel grounded, happy and have a sense of achievement about how far we have come.

Do you have voices in your head? You do! Oh that's a great relief - I thought it was only me! It is imperative that you have total belief that you will achieve what you set out to do. If the voice in your head keeps telling you that you are rubbish at negotiation, un-punctual and disorganised, you probably will be! Making a decision to become a

176

confident, well organised and professional human being is the first step to actually becoming one. If you have been on the MLCS training day and listened to my story about stammering you will know what I mean.

When we got to ten Rent to Rent properties we decided to stop and take stock. We were a little surprised to find that we suddenly had over 60 tenants and a specialist Multi-Let lettings business without the systems to support it. We like to do things well and really didn't want things to spiral out of control so we began researching and creating bigger and better systems, which we now teach on our E.D.G.E. Training, which takes you through the steps you will need to go from one or two properties to ten or twenty and turn it into a real business. We also realised that two of the first properties we had taken on were not performing as well as we had hoped for, so we made preparations to hand these back at the end of the term. This is another brilliant aspect of MLCS, if you make a mistake with area or property type or indeed landlord type, you can simply remove any furniture and fittings, hand the property back when the contract expires and move on to the next deal. We lined up two much better properties and made a seamless transition. These were better properties in every way that therefore attracted better tenants and make much better cash flow.

> *The first thing you must do is to add value and the second thing is to be profitable. Miss the first and you miss the second. Look through the eyes of your customer. Identify their problem, amplify it and then fix it, don't sell, help. By constantly adding value you will erase the competition.*

We noticed that our area in Bristol was getting somewhat swamped with people wanting to do Rent to Rent (partly my fault by selling it so well on the MLCS courses!) and agents either didn't like it and were getting fed up with saying no, or they were still saying no because they saw the power of the system and THEY are doing it themselves! (More and more agents are!) What this meant for us was that we had to regroup and rethink our strategies as how to approach agents and how we were going to position ourselves in the eyes of the property owners. This proved to be another intense time for us and we focused, I mean totally focussed, on taking things up a notch to the next level. This in turn resulted in us creating the E.D.G.E. MLCS business manual and new a training programme for serious people who really want to create a lasting business and perhaps even a legacy.

We also revisited a book called the E-Myth by Michael Gerber and tried to implement its lessons, to work on the business as opposed to in the business. The first thing we needed to do was get some help so we started advertising for a property manager. This was another learning curve for us but we learn fast and after a few false starts now have our first very valuable and trusted member of the staff. He does all the viewing, the signing in and out of the tenants and takes care of all the day to day running of the lettings side including dealing with maintenance issues. This has freed up time for us to concentrate on growing the portfolio and exploring different avenues such as buying, refurbishing, selling properties and writing books!

Diversifying the MLCS training events: we have identified that a lot of people seem to have a slight aversion to working with and dealing with agents, and we really want them to feel confident as this is an important part of the business. We decided that the best way to do this was to get a top agent working with us on the team and are lucky (!) enough to now be working in partnership with a very high profile property professional that will really help to *Turbo-Charge* the fortunes of our mentees. In fact together we have now created a very specific and confidence

178

building training day that will dig deep into how to get agents asking to work with YOU - again this is all about positioning and perception. When you continue to move forward and strive for excellence in every area, opportunities will without doubt continue to reveal themselves to you.

Momentum: For Emily and me, a really important part of building the business is to be on it each and every day, even if it's only for an hour (re The Slight Edge). As a kid did you have one of those roundabouts in your local park - the type where you hold onto the bars and scoot your foot hard to slowly pick up speed. The rides were very heavy and it was tough work getting started but as soon as you did you were off, the wind was blowing in your hair and you only had to do the occasional scoot to maintain speed, you felt like you were flying! Just about *everything* in life requires a concentrated blast of energy to get going and reach cruising speed and this especially includes starting any new business venture. It is sad to see someone feeling battered, getting disheartened and giving up just because they have received a few 'no's' from apathetic agents who didn't really understand the business model, when all they had to do was to keep going for a little while longer to hit gold.

> *Once you have achieved true momentum everything gets easier and the physics are reversed. You will start getting much more out for the effort you are putting in. Cool.*

A Support Community

... this is humongously important!

'If you want to go fast, go alone, but if you want to go far, go together'. How many people do you know that are successful in business and have got there entirely by themselves? OK there may be a few but not many, and this is true not just in business but in every area of life. Together we are stronger, everyone knows that!

We totally understand that starting out or even branching off in a new direction can be completely daunting and it's easy to become overwhelmed with the information you receive and with all the unanswered questions that spring up after you have left the training room. There is just no way anyone can possibly get all they need in the seven or so hours of a training day to enable them to set up and run a new Rent to Rent business. So we decided to do something about this and set up a support group on Facebook. It currently has over 350 members including many experienced property professionals, chartered accountants, letting and estate agents who all regularly contribute to the group. This is very powerful indeed and it should not be overlooked to have team members such as these.

> **Support System:** *Get stuck, ask a question, get the answer and become unstuck!*

180

As far as setting up a Rent to Rent business, this support is actually monstrously enormously gigantically monumentally huge and yet is often overlooked by people thinking of jumping onto a training event when they are looking at the cost. Our events are a little more expensive than other events out there but they don't offer a lifetime of consultancy within that price! Over the last few years a certain caring nature seems to have materialised within the group and it was christened by one of its founder members at the MLCS family, and that seems to fit very well. With most other events out there, as soon as the day is over and they have your money it's a case of *'Hasta la vista Baby'!*

Another unexpected bonus of the MLCS lifetime support group is that I get to constantly interact with everyone as they build their little property empires to see what is really working at grass roots level. Sometimes I don't hear anything from a person for months and then they suddenly pop up again and tell everyone they have secured four properties and are now looking at taking over a B&B! This means they have given it their total focus and are coming up for air! This is brilliant and I totally advocate it. The constant feedback as to what is working and what is not working is very useful in setting the direction of the training days which are constantly updated as the market and trends shift and move.

Bizarrely approximately 5% of people who complete our training never join the support group and that means they will not have had access to the £1,000's of contracts therein nor the interaction that is invaluable in growing their business. Why is this? Only Arthur C. Clark can answer this and he's dead.

Something we always encourage in the group is to take baby steps when starting out, as trying to master everything at the same time will often result in you becoming overwhelmed and putting the manual back up on the top shelf 'for later'. I recently heard a guy talking about this at a seminar. I enjoy spending a day or so listening to new speakers to get their take on life, on business and pick up any presentation tips. He was talking about all of us taking our first few baby steps, probably from mummy to daddy and then back again, repeated over and over again until we mastered it. He said we must do this in business or we'll end up flat on our faces and stay down there because it's easy to quit. I had visions of all the people who never ever learned to walk crawling around all over the place HeHe! A universal truth is that if you master and repeat simple steps over and over again, it will lead you to success.

Taking Action Snapshot

Inga Rasmane, Cambridge

"My area is Cambridge and I started on the 13th May 2013.

I have two big reasons; I lost a lot of money trying to invest in properties in Latvia and was feeling very down about this for about 5 years. I couldn't forgive myself etc. ... Then in 2012 I received awful news, I was diagnosed with skin cancer. That was a huge shock at first but I quickly turned it into a motivation to do something! First because I wanted to stand up and to prove to myself that I can be successful, but my even bigger reason was my son. I knew I had to do something to make him feel safe and secure for the future.

So I jumped in, took action and booked onto the MLCS course with Francis and Emily. I have now set up two Rent to Rent two properties that have a current net cash flow per month of £1,000.

My big Plan is to secure another 4 Multi-lets by the end of the year to take the portfolio up to 6 properties. With my other commitments it will be a tough goal to accomplish but I am determined.

Happiness scale; seven out of ten but it will be ten by the end of the year!"

The 5 Step Success System

... bottling up the process

My belief is that everything in life can be broken down into simple baby steps, in fact I used to apply that same thinking when I was doing my construction work. Einstein said that *if you can't explain it simply, you don't understand it well enough!* It is so easy to feel crushed and want to wave the white flag of surrender when you realise you have a mammoth task ahead of you, i.e. to quit! Emily and I have a great little mantra on a postcard in our office that says 'Change Small and Change Often'. You have probably heard the old *'How do you eat an elephant ... one bite at a time'* analogy? I have broken the MLCS process down to five straightforward steps; learning the system, planning your approach, securing a property, building your team and systemising your business. These are modules that can be mastered before you move onto the next. Each module in itself is also broken down into smaller bite sized chunks.

To get the most from the MLCS strategy there must be one person in your team that must have an all-consuming, egomaniacal, borderline obsessive, OCD, 100% belief and total trust in the process, and guess what, that person is YOU!! When you are talking to property owners and letting agents, if you have even the tiniest doubt about what you are doing this will shine through in your eyes, the words you use, your mannerisms and even your body language and start to unravel you like a ball of wool that the cats been playing with! So number one with this, or indeed any, strategy is to totally learn and internalise the information. I used to play a little game of devil's advocate with Emily where one of us would take on the role of the property owner or agent and ask the other one the most awkward or difficult question we possibly could think of. We would then analyse the answers and start over, often for hours on end. What we were doing is arming ourselves for every eventuality so that when we did approach any agents it felt like déjà vu. It was also fun to see who could ask the most awkward question. Emily always won!

Like most things in life, if you want to move from a generalist to a specialist to an authority, you must really know your subject. We have found that forward thinking agents love the system and we predict that over time old school agents will see the power of it and open their doors to it. In the meantime, you have to keep your belief and keep waving the MLCS flag. To be honest I don't really like predicting anything, especially the future!

Emily and I have come a long way in two years since the day we knocked on the door of our first agent to now being financially independent and working with some of the top professionals in the country, and there is nothing special about us - just the simple system we are using. If we were to meet two years from now, where would you be, will you be any happier? If like most people you want change for you and your family you have to get started, you have to get on the launch pad and light that fuse! So a little more digging into our simple process;

1. **Learning the system.** Time to go back to school! You could just read whenever you get a spare moment, like on the tube or at the breakfast table like you would a book (say this book). But when learning and internalising important information from the training manual it is better

184

to put aside X number of hours per day or per week and sit down with no distractions and really internalise the information. This is utterly life-changing stuff so it would be crazy not to give it your undivided attention.

2. **Planning your approach.** Let's think about this for a second. Why would any letting agent or property owner want to work with you or entrust their valuable property to you. Are you prepared? Have you done your homework? Do you have a strategic plan? What are other people's perceptions of you? Ask your friends or colleagues - make it a fun game if you like. Sharpen up your act buddy!

3. **Securing a property.** So you have been successful in your negotiations and are picking up the keys to a property that will make you £900 net per month. A few more of these and you will be able to wave bye bye to that cheap smelling heinous boss of yours. But who will be responsible for what? What contract will you be using? Will it attract VAT? What insurance will you need? You must have perfect clarity before you walk in that office to sign on the dotted line.

4. **Building your team.** Do you have any systems in place? Who can you call on for assistance? What happens when you are on holiday? What if you need a real fast room turnaround? Is paperwork really your forte? Who can you get on board? This is something you must be doing from day one and there is no need to feel overwhelmed as it is really just a tick list to ensure every base is covered. I have found that the best way to get someone to help you is to ask them! Jane has a great way to get me to do things; she says 'perhaps we should get a younger man to do it!' Sneaky!

5. **Systemising your business.** This really is my favourite bit and between Emily and I it has at times turned

185

into a game of one-upmanship to see who can create the best time and cost effective system. Subscribing to a master key system was a good contender for the number one position from Emily, but I think I am still at the top of the leader board as I can furnish an entire property extremely cheaply by making just one 60 second phone call. I don't even have to touch the furniture - it just arrives in the house! This is just one of the many really cool systems we have put into place, and they all make up parts of the larger MLCS jigsaw. 5 or 10 parts of a 200 piece jigsaw aren't really of much use on their own but we have all the pieces.

Taking Action Snapshot

Elliot Hughes, London

I started off with Rent to Rent as I had no money and it worked well for me and created good cash flow. As I was then seen to be active in the industry, I was offered £100k by an investor and started sourcing and buying HMO's. Because I was able to find good deals, more people offered me more money and it's gone from there. The MLCS training with Francis and Emily was invaluable for me as I really got to understand the business principles of running and managing Multi-Lets. Francis has sent many local people my way for help and they too are now getting some great results.

Recently I've had someone come to me asking for help in West London and it looks like we shall do a joint venture where I'll give him the knowledge, the business support of dealing with agents and how to run HMOs etc and in return he's going to do all the leg-work with the day to day management. This is very new so let's see how it goes. I would say that even if you don't do actual Rent to Rent, the training is essential for how to efficiently run a HMO. Highly recommended.

Happiness scale out 10 would be a 9! (Always room for improvement! haha)

The MLCS Springboard

... and Joint Ventures

Did you ever climb to the highest springboard in your local swimming pool? I did, once! When I got there I realised it was much higher than I had mentally prepared for and there was not a chance in hell was I going to dive off it headfirst! So after hanging around for a while pretending to be admiring the view with a death grip on the safety rail, I had the humiliating task of climbing back down the ladder past smirking little whippersnappers half my age. Doh!

What is the purpose of a spring board? To propel you further and faster than you are able to go on your own. I have lost count of the offers of joint ventures we have had since we started gaining some success with Rent to Rent and we were shoved into the spotlight. This goes for lots of guys in the MLCS group as well because as soon as people see that you are active, that you know your stuff and are getting results you will attract joint venture opportunities. If you have a good deal the money, will show up. Some will be good for you and will drive your business forward; some may not so good so it's up to you to pick and choose what will work. Don't always focus on the monetary gain as making sure you are congruent is just as important as the air you are presently breathing. We are currently doing three separate joint ventures.

I was reading a Facebook thread where I was referred to as the Multi-Let Rent to Rent expert. I wondered how I got there and thought to myself that an expert is just someone who has made all the mistakes that can be made in a narrow field. Like Thomas Edison, you can fail your way to success, and that is pretty much what I have done. When you start out you know very little, so if you are smart you read all you can on the subject, you listen to audios, watch DVDs, go to seminars and soak it all up like a sponge. Then when you have all the pieces of the jigsaw in your head you must rearrange them to make sense of it all and find a place and an order for everything. Like Edison I never think of anything as a failure, just another way that didn't work as you plough on to find the way that does work.

Even though Rent to Rent has now survived for well over 20 years, somebody recently told me with highly enthusiastic glee that it wouldn't be around in 5 years' time and therefore I would be out of a job (another case of crabs in the barrel). I told them that I got out of a J.O.B. years ago and have many other interests and investment strategies including buying and holding large Multi-Let properties. Setting up a Rent to Rent business has certainly opened others doors and created many opportunities for us and it will do the same for you too with the connections you make along the way. So don't think too small, make big goals - where do you want to be in 10 years' time? We have already done, and are planning more joint ventures with people who even a year ago I thought were in another league to us. I was thinking small. I recently heard a talk by a gentleman about not being confined to small deals and small thinking, and after doing a quick survey of the room it became evident that his one last deal would generate enough cash flow per month to allow over 50% of the audience to become financially independent. The downside is that he was an experienced investor and that deal would have scared the pants off most people. But in reality it's only numbers, either they add up or they don't.

The Age of the Entrepreneur

... gaining the E.D.G.E.

We are entering into the age of the Entrepreneur - have we come a full circle? Remember the nursery rhyme - the butcher, the baker, the candle-stick maker? These people were all entrepreneurs in their own right. Today there is a different type of entrepreneur.

If you lived in the agricultural age you probably ate whatever you grew and if you had a good crop you sold or traded the rest. If you lived in the industrial age you more than likely got a job in the local factory and never wandered far from home. Then along came the wonderful information age with every bit of knowledge in the world at your fingertips (although when we look back this may also become known as the age of distraction! I have been recently turning off my mobile phone when I really need to focus, shock horror!) I truly believe that we are now entering into the age of the entrepreneur with little micro industries opening up all over the planet. This has in part been possible by the arrival of personal computers with more capacity than Nasa had to get their rockets into space in the 1960's! Look how much the world has changed since computers first entered our homes in the 1980's, since Google arrived on the scene in 1998 and Facebook burst into existence in 2004! I am a big fan of cloud technology which I have been using for several years. This allows me to instantly and easily share selected information with people I work with in my immediate and extended team.

Clouds: Using Egnyte.com has made our systems so much easier to use at so many levels. If you are not sure what I am talking about or think that clouds are fluffy things that float in the sky, think again! If you are not sure how to set it up on your computer, outsource it - that is what we are talking about here. You can find skilled workers at websites like Fiverr.com, PeoplePerhour.com but first perhaps ask your young niece or nephew? So my own little revolution was cloud technology, if you are not using cloud technology you need to switch over right now! You will love it.

It's like unstoppable little bush fires of brilliance are flaring up all over the planet, all of which can tap straight into the global market to catapult them forward. Suddenly resources that were once unimaginable are freely available. I had a great little high quality 2 minute promotional video made for $5, this is incredible value. I also have instant access to members of 'my' team in India, the Philippines, Brazil, America and in fact all over the world! I use them on an *ad hoc* basis as and when I need them to do jobs that I neither have the time or skills to do. You just have to make sure you understand each other and are both reading from the same hymn sheet before you get started (a voice of experience). I also have to be aware of time-zones and not upset my man in America again with a 3 a.m. call!!

There has never been a better time in history to embrace entrepreneurialism with so many tools, opportunities and so much technology at our fingertips. You can create a website that is every bit as professional as the big corporate companies of old and be more competitive than those companies. Working for yourself is more fun as you get to choose when you work, where you work and who you work with. I am typing this sentence sat by a lake with a cool breeze blowing!

192

Whether we like it or not the world will keep spinning and change is inevitable. I can recall as a boy hearing disgruntled adults having conversations about their jobs being replaced by machines. Computers seem to have been welcomed by most - except for my neighbour Barry who still complains about them a lot! We can waste energy fighting the march of technology or we can embrace and I usually choose to go for the embrace! What I don't understand I simply get some help with until outsourcing has become a habit.

> ***The one that will make you rich:*** *Leverage, Manage, Automate, Do!*

On a recent trip to Ireland I did a little research of the family. I was pleased to discover my Grandparents were also entrepreneurs. They had 11 children, 10 that survived to adulthood my mother being the youngest. They took care of all their own needs and were the very first people in the district to acquire a radio and then a gramophone, which would attract the neighbours from far and wide to listen to Frank Sinatra and his peers each and every Saturday night. My Grandfather was a farmer and a fisherman and they made all their own clothes. I visited their grave by the coast in Galway and laid some flowers; we all want to know where we came from.

The word entrepreneur scares some people - the thought of stepping out of a well- paid or even not so well-paid job. I have been self-employed and working for myself for so long I just cannot envisage ever working for someone else again. In fact I got the sack from the last three jobs I worked in - I think the universe was trying to tell me something. The last time this happened was when I was arguing with an arrogant and explosive boss who screamed in my face 'Francis, this is not some silly pantomime', to which of course I was compelled to reply 'o-h y-e-s it is! I collected my coat on the way out.

Working for yourself forces you to get your head down and get the job done, because if you don't perform or you get lazy, the only person who is going to suffer the consequences is you and your family. You can define your own life and live by your own rules but you will need to Focus, Focus, Focus and get the job done! Who is in charge now? You are, this is your time, the age of the entrepreneur!

Taking Action Snapshot

Suzanne Mullen, London

"I started my Rent to Rent journey in November 2013 after I watched Francis and Emily's webinar, and then attended his course. I am a full time Mum and looking for a way to earn income whilst also doing the school run. Rent to Rent seemed like the perfect option for me and to be honest at first even seemed too good to be true! After meeting Francis though, I gained the belief that it was possible and sprung straight into action!

My primary aim was to make the strategy work as close to my home as possible, and concentrate mainly in the Haringey area of North London. Fairly soon after my training I secured a property with £500+ cash flow and have another 2 on the same road I am currently negotiating for. One of these deals will cash flow £1,300 a month. It is all very exciting!

My plan for the future is to secure at least another 5 properties and a net cash flow of £5,000 per month. Looking at the bigger picture, my aim is to start buying multi-lets, which now seems very achievable. Thank you to Francis, Emily and the MLCS team, I am happier than I have ever been and no longer worry about my financial future.

On a scale of happiness, I am currently at 8 with 10 in sight! Thank you for opening my eyes to all the opportunities available.

Taking (Massive) Action

... it's easier than you think

Have you ever been on a Roller-coaster ride? I paid a visit to a good friend in Florida and eventually found myself standing beneath the shadow of a metal beast of a ride. I don't recall what it was called, probably *Convulsion* or *Haemorrhage* or something like that. My friend had been inferring that I was a big sissy for not wanting to at least have one go after coming all this way! We had got to the park early and were near the front of the queue. I shuffled along getting closer and closer knowing that I could back out at any time (sound familiar?) We got to the gate and I hesitated. My friend looked at me and raised his left eyebrow in such a condescending manner that it made me draw back my shoulders, stride across to the metal devil and get myself strapped in. I'm no sissy ... at least I don't think so?

At that time I was experiencing a myriad of emotions - fear, excitement, grim resignation and to be truthful even a little sissy boy panic (but I would never admit that publicly). This was my first time and I told myself it was perfectly natural to be feeling this way - in fact it would be weird if I was not. My friend was talking but I could only half focus, most of my brain was working overtime trying to think how to get out of this situation whilst retaining my dignity. Maybe I could suddenly remember that I had a pace-maker fitted last week? Too late, we were moving!

The chairs began to tip forward. OMG we are facing the ground and moving forward at speed, over the metal floor, over the safety net, getting higher and higher as the ground disappears below us. I am very tense and not really enjoying this at all, what if the safety harness fails, or the wheels come off the track and splatter me like strawberry jam all over the tarmac below, but too late now to stop and go back. This was a bad idea and I will be glad when it is over! My roller-coaster veteran friend could sense my tension (maybe it was my high pitched wailing and rapid breathing) and having ridden many a wild twisty turny beast, he knew exactly what to do, he said four words that changed everything, *'relax and enjoy it'*. So I did. I took a few long slow breaths and relaxed and what a blast it was! I just went with the flow and felt like a little kid again, it was exhilarating! We got off and guess what; yes I wanted to go again! What had I been afraid of, I had conquered my fears and it was an amazing experience!

Ok here comes the forced and tenuous analogy: training, buying property, networking events, you name it, we all feel anxious and even a little panic when we are doing something for the first time. We envisage everything that will go wrong. (I had accepted that I was going to die on that rollercoaster!) But often when we actually do it, it turns out to be fun and we wonder what all the fuss was about. Then after a short time you 'own' it and walk into that room with confidence and wonder why the newbies are all so nervous! This is human nature.

I actually had a few more goes on the rollercoasters before I flew home and it got better each time - I guess I knew what to expect and was more confident and relaxed. How would I have felt if I had bottled it and came home with my tail between my legs? Like a sissy for sure and every time I saw a rollercoaster or indeed my friend I would have been reminded of a missed opportunity. Regret

197

is a horrible emotion that will gnaw away at you for years and to be avoided at all costs.

Most experienced investors would say that 'right now' is the perfect time to get into property; if you know what you are doing you can make money in any market. It's true that there is no time like the present to take action and get started no matter what is going on in the economy, but for Multi-Let properties this is especially true - the stars really are all in alignment! There are many reasons for this - banks are still not lending, there is a tightening of mortgage criteria and ongoing job instability. Add to this the constant immigration that the UK is experiencing and the never ending housing shortage and what we have is a golden opportunity for those investing in Multi-Let properties, whether it's to buy or to control them - for us, this is like the perfect storm!

You may have noticed at the start of this book I made a dedication to the memory of my good friend Pete. He was a well-read man and was really looking forward to delving into the completed manuscript of this book, as he had gently given me many pointers as to what he considered to be my good ideas and which ideas should be allocated a permanent place in the dark recesses of my mind (and there were many). Pete felt like he had been let down by the system as he knew something was seriously wrong with him but he was fobbed off for many months by an incompetent doctor who was just cruising into retirement. Consequently his diagnosis and treatment came very late, too late for Pete. Can money buy you health and happiness? Well it could have bought Pete a BUPA appointment within 24 hours and who knows; perhaps he would still be with us now instead of buried in a cardboard box in the woods (his last request which took a lot of organising I can tell you!)

Pete didn't drive and was very selective about whom he spent his time with; especially when he knew that his time was short. When the hospital appointments eventually came through he asked me to make the round trips with him. We lived a way apart and this would mean taking the most part of a day as we would always go for lunch in Pete's favourite pie shop. Homemade pie, a few fat chips and a cup of tea while we talked passionately about the authentic blues music that we both loved. We did this many times and I also visited Pete at his house where we sat and talked and played his latest Ray Wiley Hubbard rare American import. One time when I was driving home I thought to myself that I had achieved what I had set out to do three years earlier - to be a master of my own time and not have to drag myself off to work for some nameless entity anymore. In fact after setting my alarm clock for 6.30 a.m. for 20 years, these days I only ever set it if I need to catch an early flight. (I'm sure if God had wanted us to fly he would have made it easier to get to the airport!)

How did I do it? By selecting a system that I knew would work, by sticking to a plan of action, by turning off the white noise of the world for a while and staying focused, by adopting a can-do attitude, by soaking up information, by mixing with the right people and by not giving up, even when it got really tough. It's just a process but you have got to really want to do it. You have got to find your burning reason to jump out of bed each and every morning and dive into your work like a squirrel with his tail on fire. (OK. Bad analogy!) All the little moments and scenes of our lives add up to make a movie. What's yours like. Will it be worth watching? Will it have a happy ending? It's not about the big stuff; it's about the hundreds of little things you choose to do every day and the setting of a thousand suns -The Slight Edge is always at work.

If we have not already, I hope we get to work together and maybe I can help you build a profitable Rent to Rent business that may just change your life. If not, then I truly hope this book has helped you in some small way and will at least set you on the path. Remember, all you have to do is to take action and never lose sight of what you want to accomplish! Carpe Diem!

Taking Action Snapshot

Peter Savage, Somerset

"I first started investing in property in 2011. I was completely new to property and realised that there is so much to be learn. I first met Fran and Emily and went on the MLCS course last year. Since then I have taken on 8 Rent to Rents. This has been an enormous benefit to my wealth strategy, it's given me cash flow, it's given me a lot of experience in managing lettings and has enabled me to progress quicker than I would have done if I'd just been waiting and saving up for a deposit to buy my next property. This has been one of the many steps I have needed and I've learnt masses. It's a very very informative course where you can learn step by step how to get started into your journey into property investment.

Happiness scale out of ten: nine at the moment as I'm still getting there!"

Training and Mentoring

... pay now or pay for it later

So why commit to any training at all when you can do it all by yourself. There is a great analogy I picked up somewhere along the line about trying to chop down a big old tree with a blunt axe. A smart person will spend a good portion of the time sharpening the axe and preparing for the job in hand, whereas a foolish person will pick up the blunt axe and immediately start swinging wildly at the tree. What do you think will happen? Without the correct tools and preparation even a simple job can seem impossible and it's no wonder then that these foolish people throw in the towel and give up. Which type of person are you? Do you work smart or just 'work'?

It is really important to use your short time on the planet wisely and keep learning and growing until the day you take your final breath. It's also important that you mix with people you admire and who are already doing what you aspire to do. It is said that we are the product of the five people we spend the most time with! Who do you spend your time with? You should try to be the dumbest person in your immediate networking group (this has never been a problem for me!)

When you are planning your trainings, do your research carefully and consider if you are congruent with the trainers and their companies philosophies. Do they have real testimonials and a proven track record? Check you can free up space in your diary and check your life plans to make sure you will have time to absorb and implement what you learn, or there really is no point to it. Don't grab at it, rather grow into it.

Emily and I created the MLCS training day as an introduction to Rent to Rent and as a springboard to building a Multi Let property portfolio. We realise that everyone is different with different needs, and so have now developed a series of training days and events to ensure that everyone gets exactly what they need to kick-start their property investing career.

Whatever path you choose, I solemnly encourage you to pick one strategy, stay focused on your destination and I guarantee that you'll get there. But don't forget to stop for the occasional glass of champagne along the way! Good luck.

Would you like to Turbo Charge your cash-flow with Multi Lets?

Check out our website for a fuller explanation of how we do it:

www.MultiLetCashflowSystem.com

✓ Download our free training videos
✓ Attend one of our energised training days
✓ Find out how you can set up systems and processes
✓ How you can avoid the common mistakes
✓ It is described as a complete business in a box
✓ We have an extensive step by step manual
✓ Flash-drives with all documentation needed
✓ See how you can recycle your deposit again and again
✓ Why Multi Lets and especially Rent to Rent is a growth industry
✓ Gain access to a lifetime 24/7 dynamic support community

✓ Read that last line a few times!

You may also want to check out my personal website where you will find an abundance (there's that word again) of very useful Rent to Rent/Multi-Let video blogs, and the MMM website where you will find waiting for you in the high security MMM strong-room, the missing Chapter 50, plus links to all the resources mentioned in this book, plus many highly compromising photos of all of its contributors!

www.FrancisDolley.com

www.MayhemMurderandMultiLets.com

You will also be able to access a pre-recorded Rent to Rent webinar that will cover:

✓ Training: How to decide on your point of entry
✓ Opening for business - 3 solid foundation principles
✓ Working with agents - the 5 main reasons some investors fail
✓ How to easily pinpoint the perfect Rent to Rent property
✓ The fastest way to build a solid Rent to Rent income
✓ How to implement the 5 Step MLCS Success System
✓ Video blog with Francis & Emily, but who's interviewing who?

What drives some people forward with new ideas and business while others plod along happily in their world and their J.O.B's, seemingly oblivious to the oncoming doom?
Why is it that some people suddenly burst into action as if they had been struck by a thunderbolt? A life

shattering experience perhaps or just out of sheer desperation?

Whatever you decide to do after reading this book, please don't let a 'good' life get in the way of living a 'great' life, and remember to *TAKE ACTION* and move towards your goals each and every day!

Francis' Next Book

Turbo-Charge Your Cashflow
with Multi-Lets

Mayhem, Murder & Multi-Lets was not the book I had intended to write at all. I had been researching and preparing a book with a working title of *'Turbo-Charge Your Cashflow with Multi-Lets.'* A little way into that process I was in the bar area of a Holiday Inn after a local property meet, chatting with some people about our experiences as landlords. My 'Mayhem' stories brought forth so many outbursts of emotion that they insisted I turn it into a talk to present to the group in a few months' time, which I did and the MMM talk and consequently this book, were born. I have heard it said that writing a book is like having a baby and I don't want MMM to be an only child, so have decided to now crack on with *'Turbo-Charge'!*

Turbo-Charge is a series of in depth interviews with some of the most experienced Multi-Let investors working in the UK today and for a balanced view, a few people who are right at the start of their property investing journey (I am currently taking bribes if you want to be included!). It documents how they started, how they overcame the inevitable challenges they faced along the way, where they are now and what they would do differently. Most importantly for many readers I asked the question of everyone; If you were starting out again today with limited funds, what would you do. Their answers surprised, sometimes even amazed me but always totally inspired me.

You can subscribe to our free Rent to Rent property training videos and occasional newsletter, and check out video blogs of a different kind at the websites below. You can also follow us on Facebook to keep up to date with current developments.

www.MultiLetCashflowSystem.com

www.FrancisDolley.com

About Francis

Francis has property in his blood and has always loved everything about it from the construction styles to the history and the evolution. It was only recently, after being dragged onto a stage, that he realised he also enjoyed teaching people what he knew. He loves seeing the change in people he has helped when they break free of their old lives and embrace the wonderful world of financial independence that Multi Let properties can very swiftly create. As he says *'It's like a light comes on and a passion wells up inside them'*.

Francis has taught hundreds of people the Multi-Let Cashflow System, which in turn has helped them to 'Turbo-Charge' their cash-flow. As one happy student said *"Francis is changing people's lives for the better"*

He has spoken to audiences of over a thousand at property conferences in Wembley Stadium and shared the stage with the likes of Bob Geldof, Alan Sugar and James Caan.

Moving into the training room circuit, Francis was well aware of how tedious some training events can be and so designed his to be anything but that. Delegates can never believe how fast the day goes! Everyone who attends gets everything they need to set up a high-cash flowing Rent to Rent business and most importantly of all, they also get lifetime support - something Francis is passionate about.

As he says 'I understand why other trainers don't do this as it takes a huge amount of our time and effort but we believe it's a service every course provider should be offering and will continue to do so.'

As for the future; Francis will continue to slowly build his portfolio one property at a time whilst expanding and improving the training events to ever higher standards. As well as the introduction to Rent to Rent day there is now also a mentorship programme and the popular 'working with letting agents' day. He is also building working partnerships and affiliations with some of the country's leading property professionals.

Francis' final words. Why do we all do the things we do? I have always been driven by wanting to give my family a good home and an interesting life away from the usual hum drum. Would I have achieved half of the things I have done without my wife Jane and children James and Emily? Not a chance! They are hardworking, focused and adaptable and I'm lucky to have them on my 'team'. So from the bottom of my heart I want to say thank you for your love and understanding, your constant encouragement and support and for unequivocally keeping my feet on the ground. Without you, there would have been no point at all. We still have a lot of memories to make together and lots of photo frames to fill, so let's get busy!'

....
....
.... phew!

Wishing you health, wealth & happiness from

Francis, Jane, James & Emily

Printed in Great Britain
by Amazon.co.uk, Ltd.,
Marston Gate.